Pretty Good Advice

for People Who
DREAM BIG
and
WORK HARDER

Leslie Blodgett

Abrams Image, New York

*To all bareMinerals employees
and customers,
past, present, and future.*

Pretty
Good
Advice

Advice is tricky. Giving it can come off a little high-handed, especially when you're offering it up to people you don't know. And taking it can be equally risky. Just because it worked for the person shelling it out, that doesn't mean it will work for you.

I get all that, 'cause, honestly, I never give advice. Welcome to my book, *Pretty Good Advice*. My possibly flawed logic:

1. I've gained some pretty juicy insights based on decades of being alive.
2. Since I never give advice to strangers, I am going to pretend that we're good friends.
3. And since we're good friends, I know you are only going to take what you need and skip the boring parts.

Beauty
Is
Generous

1. As they were taking the bandages off Janet Tyler's face, the nurses looked on with dread. This was the eleventh surgery attempt to make her look normal. As the final bandage was lifted, the nurses shrieked, "No! No! It didn't work!" The poor woman was the same "twisted lump of flesh" that had arrived at the hospital the first time.

Janet was traumatized. She was still Janet, blond with petite features, smooth skin, and sculpted eyebrows. Her doctor and nurses? They had the faces of monsters. That's because they were in *The Twilight Zone*. "Eye of the Beholder" was my favorite episode.

There was no shortage of women on TV looking like Janet and not like me growing up, and I idolized every one of them. But, lucky for me, all it took was a little science fiction to make me question everything. Early on I started to wonder who gets to decide who is beautiful.

The media has a lot to say about it. They put pictures in our heads to influence our thoughts and convince us they are right. They push their standards of beauty because that works—it sells stuff, and we eat it up. But the version of beauty we see all the time is just one part of the story.

I have seen trends come and go, and I have witnessed the low self-esteem that results from constantly seeing these hard-to-avoid images of so-called beauty. I've been there too. There was a time when I used to hope my legs would grow longer and my nose would shrink. Prizing certain body shapes and facial features is a fabricated construct that society is feeding us. No way am I going to look like them. And why should I?

Here is something I know. Being in the beauty industry for four decades, I have had the privilege to travel widely and meet thousands of women one-on-one. Not from a stage looking at a mass of people, but in person. So close I could count their eyelashes. I have seen so many interpretations of "beautiful" that it would take your breath away, because it has for me. I have had no choice but to expand my own vision of what beauty is just by looking around me and studying faces. (I'm not stalking you; it's admiration.) Faces hold truths, they tell of life experiences, they reveal character and express emotion.

The most compelling story of beauty is its generosity. It's not restrictive, not exclusive. The more you see it, the more you understand it. And understanding leads to caring about other people

8

and their journey. It also leads to caring more about yourself.

Don't believe everything they tell you about what is or isn't beautiful. It's horsefeathers. The more beauty you see in the world, the more beautiful you become.

Makeup Has Your Back

2. I was thirteen. Full metal braces with springy rubber bands, zits on my forehead, and hair that didn't follow instructions. It was game day. I was on the junior high school kickline, and I had just finished putting on my blue eyeshadow and pink frosty lip balm. I looked in the mirror and gave myself a thumbs-up. I walked into the kitchen, where Mom was cooking French toast for her most recent "gentleman friend." He looked up from the paper and said, "Don't worry, kid, you'll be pretty someday."

What a freakin' jerk.

After I'd pulled the knife out of my heart, I decided it didn't matter what that jerk thought. I loved how makeup made me feel, how it covered my zits and made my eyes sparkle, and mostly how it was a way to express myself. I was no Farrah Fawcett, but I was my own version of pretty.

Me, circa the French toast incident

Daydreaming Is Working on Stuff

3. I was so skilled at daydreaming as a kid that at times I feared I would fall headfirst into a fantasy and miss dinner. My most prolific sessions were sitting in the backseat of the car, leaning into the window with the sun rays beating me into a trance. I would be living it up in my head: winning at track meets, speaking fluent Spanish, performing onstage without a hitch.

In the 1980s, I heard that such imagining had a name: "creative visualization." This technique looks a lot like spacing out. So, naturally, people you live with may accuse you of being a sloth, but that couldn't be further from the truth. You are working on stuff. Daydreaming is a mystery trip with no goal and no destination. Who knows where you will wind up? Your imagination is boss. Nowadays, for me, it's like taking a nap with the Dalai Lama or Bradley Cooper (well, as long as I'm taking a nap with people).

If someone in your home tells you to "snap out of it," refuse.

Tell them you're in a meeting of the mind.

First Jobs
Build
Character

4. The minute I turned sixteen, I got my first (real) job, one where I paid taxes and got $.25 raises. I adored my blue polyester pantsuit* with fabric that breathed like a dragon. I was employed part-time at McDonald's, where I worked my way up from sweeping the parking lot to cooking burgers. I learned a ton, like how to upsell the apple pie. Sure, I was covered in grease after my shift. But the experience stuck with me. I could absolutely make a Big Mac today (and I can still sing the Big Mac song). One of my favorite things about the job—besides the outstanding teamwork and crushing the high-action lunch rush—was that I learned from a co-worker how to do the multi-eyeshadow application technique using muted shades of purple. And I pierced someone's ear during my lunch break.

Take pride in your first job.

* *I worked at two different McDonald's, which meant two different uniforms—one hamburger brown, and the other powder blue. And we had hats.*

Ramble, Sometimes

5. In the 1960s, my dad drove a black Rambler with a red interior. We didn't wear seat belts back then, and there was a nice-sized hole in the floor. It was so cool: When we looked down, we could see the street speeding beneath us on our way to Buddy Burgers. "Rambler" was an odd name for a car. Definition of "ramble" from the internet: "Move aimlessly or without any specific destination, often in search of food or employment." This did not describe my dad; he was a beloved high school biology teacher and the most fun dad on the block. He would sing and dance in the grocery store, teach us how to sketch comic book characters, and bring home candy on Friday nights.

Best dad ever. Everyone loved Dad.

Except Mom. They were divorced in 1972, one month before my tenth birthday. While my mother was freed from the confines of an unpredictable husband who did things like buy a used car with a hole in the floor, we kids were stunned by the sudden turn of events. It was a confusing next couple of years (decades), because he loved his kids more than life. But he chose to leave for good. The divorce was never discussed, and we were expected to carry on. Some people would call that cruel—and I would say, yep, it was cruel—but we all learned to develop coping mechanisms.

Like keeping busy. My school days were full. Idling wasn't an option. Being busy filled my time, but the minute I left home for college, I lost my way. I knew I was off track, but I couldn't steer my way back. Until a few years later, when, with my mother's nudging, I found some direction.*

And while I have tried my best to forget those times, I own them now. If you find you're out there rambling, don't feel bad about it. It doesn't have to stop your journey; it can just be part of it—left turns included.

See Nº6. Thanks, Mom.

Thanks, Mom

6. Moms sometimes have a funny way of showing they care. After two years of college, I moved to Florida for a few months. (I didn't drop out; I just decided not to go back.) I needed fresh air and time to think before I could imagine my path forward. One evening, after a long shift at the Ponderosa Steakhouse, I opened this letter:

> *Dear Leslie,*
>
> *Consider what you will do if FIT doesn't work out for you next fall. Do you have an alternative plan? You'd better think about it, or you'll be working as a waitress all your life. How does that sound?*
>
> *All for now.*
>
> > *Love,*
> > *Mom*

The truth is: I've spent most of my life trying not to disappoint my mother, and that has actually turned out to be pretty good motivation. Also, she was right. What was I doing with my life?

The sweetest pic I could find of Mom and me

Lower Your Bar

7. I like my bars low, where I can see them—and clear them. Strangely enough, I was also the queen of the limbo—the only time it is OK for your friends to chant, "How low can you go?" I actually have two pictures of me mid-limbo: one from my birthday party circa 1970, and the other from my honeymoon, with me wearing a red bikini on a pirate ship in Antigua.* The limbo is not easy—it takes flexibility, concentration, and strategy, all good skills for excelling in life.

I like my bar in view instead of in the constellations. I like to see where I'm headed, so I can plan my attack and make my move.

So decide where you like your bar. I totally appreciate how a high bar is motivational for some people, but I like the momentum of making progress. Set your own bar, a bar you can reach. Then another. And another. And guess what we just made? A ladder.

Now, you can go as high as YOU want.

* DO NOT allow anyone to take photos of you doing the limbo. Especially if you are good at it.

Get
Desperate

8. Because of my obsession with all things beauty, Mom convinced me to apply to the new Cosmetics and Fragrance Marketing program at the Fashion Institute of Technology (FIT) in New York City. I didn't get in, because I didn't have any beauty industry experience. This problem wasn't as easy to solve as you'd think. The Dior counter wouldn't hire me because I didn't have any beauty experience. Bloomingdale's wouldn't hire me because I didn't have any beauty experience.

What's a beauty hopeful supposed to do in this chicken-and-egg scenario? The obvious. I stood outside the Bloomingdale's buying office door every morning for a week. It was inconvenient for everyone involved. A narrow hallway led to the office, so the buyers had to brush by me to get to work every day. They finally hired me (to make me go away from that hallway, I think). They offered me a job selling Mei Fa Hairstyx on the cosmetics floor with no hourly wage, just a 21 percent commission on sales. I took the job, ate a lot of popcorn for dinner that year, and then FIT accepted me.

Don't
Play
Dead

9. Manhattan in the eighties was wild and overzealous in the makeup department. Especially cheeks. I spent 60 percent longer than I do now on my makeup application in those days. And then along came the nineties. Color was fading from the face, because we were supposed to look dead, remember? Extremely hip . . . but dead. I've always been a fan of looking alive.

Don't play dead. Wear blush.

Blush, like other makeup, has its trendy moments. But no matter what, I take it seriously.

How to Wear Blush:

1. If you are going to an eighties party, wear a shade of fuchsia and apply liberally.
2. If you want to look like you just came off the mountain skiing in Aspen, wear your blush on the apples of your cheeks.
3. If you want to leave work early because you're "not feeling well," don't wear blush.

Commit to Your Passion

10. News flash. Following your passion is in the doghouse these days. The idea being that you may be barking up the wrong tree, limiting yourself to a singular focus and therefore missing far-ranging opportunities that could lead to lifelong success and happiness.

I know what the researchers are saying about the downside of pursuing your passion. Because many people have no idea what their passion is, and trying to find one when you haven't a clue can just make you feel worse and waste your time. So if you aren't delirious about something right now, don't worry too much.

But if you are, and it keeps nagging at you like robocalls trying to sell you a new credit card with lower interest rates, then maybe it is time to pay attention.

I've loved makeup and beauty products since, oh, fifth grade, when I would ask for a particular fragrance for my birthday. Beauty was unquestionably, hands-down, my passion, and I followed it with the help of my mother, who was tired of me not committing already to this whole passion thing.

If you are obsessed with something, it could very well mean you have a passion for it, and you can test that theory by committing* to it. And if you don't like commitment, scrap the passion idea and go to school and learn lots of stuff.

Me in my evening face mask in the eighties

*Dictionary definition: The act of binding yourself (intellectually or emotionally) to a course of action.

Don't Sell, Serve

11. After years of mixing my shampoos in the shower and spending all my babysitting money on makeup, I finally landed my dream job: as a beauty advisor at Macy's—the Miracle on 34th Street, where I could learn from the best.

On my first day, the assistant manager showed me the ropes: sell stuff and make a 3 percent commission; sell the expensive stuff that didn't sell well and get $5 for each item; consistently sell as many products as could fit into a large shopping bag and eventually get a raise. She handed me a training manual and sent me on my way.

Turns out, the staffers were not the friendliest people. Two of my co-workers had begun a feud ten years earlier and hadn't spoken since. They marked their territories, never smiled, and if you got within two feet of their borders, you would be tarred and feathered for dipping into their rent money.

Even for the friendly ones, it was all about the commission. The thrill was in the sale. "I know I look twenty-five, but I am actually thirty," said one of my co-workers as she was pitching an anti-aging eye cream. She was twenty-three.

The customers had no idea what was happening behind the counter. Most women came in to find a new lip color and maybe to learn a makeup lesson or two, or they just wanted a break after a long day at work. They believed the well-rehearsed lines, and why wouldn't they? So they handed over their credit cards.

It was dishonest and yucky. And I learned something that has lasted me for decades. I don't want to be "good at selling." You can keep that title. It's a privilege to *serve* people. And to do that well, I need to believe in what I am doing. Simple.

You Never
Know
Where
You'll
Encounter
Love

12. If I didn't love makeup, Keith wouldn't be my husband. We met while I was working behind the Ultima II counter at Macy's. His girlfriend was my co-worker. Keith was one of the good guys. He would come before closing to pick her up so she wouldn't have to ride the subway to Brooklyn by herself at night.

I didn't steal him away or anything dramatic, but he did think I was pretty cute, or he wouldn't have called me out of the blue two years later "to say hi" after they broke up. (Let's just say I *was* super cute—see photo on page 33—and I rocked the natural look.*)

"Keith who?" I asked.

"Blodgett, Keith Blodgett."

"Who?"

Eventually I remembered, and we set our first date. I marked it in my day planner. (Those were little books with calendars that you used with a pencil or pen.) But planners were only as reliable as the person remembering to write plans in them. Suffice it to say, I was guilty of double booking. At the door that evening was Keith with a bottle of wine and a beautiful bouquet of flowers. Next to

* *For the record, "the natural look" in 1980s New York City was taking a stroll through Central Park and looking at a bush.*

him was a guy I'd met at a dance club a few nights earlier. Dance-club guy was empty-handed.

Keith and I had a great time at a cozy French restaurant. We talked about our childhoods and our taste in music (I was Punk, he was Rock), and then he did something that no one had ever dared do before . . . he insisted on picking up the tab. I was insanely frugal back then (I would use one disposable razor all year); however, on dates either I paid for the meal in full or we dined Dutch. Keith didn't speak Dutch. I let him pay. Was it because he charmed me in his sexy leather jacket? (See photo.) All I know is that the brainwashing I had received from Mom about avoiding men who wanted to control you with their wallets was beginning to seem like a bunch of hogwash. I think the technique Keith employed was called "chivalry"— and I liked it. He also opened doors and let me eat off of his plate.

A few months in, we were engaged,** and, six months later, we were married. You could call it kismet, my mother called it impulsive, but actually it was more instinctual. Because, besides being

---

** *I had a panic attack (unfortunately, a common occurrence in those days) while we were on the subway heading downtown, and we ended up in the Diamond District. A ring was purchased.*

a selfless, kind human being, Keith smelled like butter cookies. All the time, and to this day.

It's a sweet story with a couple of takeaways:

1. I'm lucky, because makeup had my back again; it got Keith and me into the same room, thus finding me a husband who smells like heaven on earth.
2. Chivalry is a form of respect—and respect is the basis of any good relationship.

Keith and me, totally on trend in the eighties

Be a
Little
Out
There

13. I'm still not sure what motivated me to send a memo outlining the astrological makeup of the employees at Neutrogena to the head of HR. Other than the fact that I was *really* into astrology. I was no Ronald Reagan (who not only became president but also consulted his astrologer on matters from scheduling the State of the Union address to the flight times of Air Force One), but I too planned around the stars. I had a Libra friend who was calm under pressure, and I decided, *I want one of those.* Keith didn't need to know why there was such urgency around conceiving a child in late January.*

I couldn't prevent my love of horoscopes from spilling over into my professional life. "So, what day and month were you born?" I would ask candidates in their job interviews. They didn't even have to tell me their sign. I knew them all. Geminis are super creative, Sagittariuses love an adventure, and Leos like to work out. The ones who joined the company got the message that the place didn't take itself too seriously, unless, of course, you were a Scorpio. They were a little intense. Calm down, I

* *Trent is a Libra.*

wasn't too tyrannical, and I didn't let it cloud my judgment (at work).

Sure, it could be a little dicey to go all woo-woo at the office, but I like being a little unpredictable. Bringing the unexpected to work is bold—ask any Aries.

```
TO:       Martine

FR:       Leslie A. Blodgett

RE:       Neutrogena News

cc:       Stephanie
```

Addendum to your segment on the Virgo luncheon:

Now for some interesting Neutrogena facts. Did you know that
Neutrogena is heavy on Fire signs and low on earth signs? Did
you know that this company is being run by Sagitarius? See
below for the astrological make-up of the employees here at
Neutrogena.

```
       Aries          7%      fire     27%
       Taurus         7%      earth    23%
       Gemini         8%      water    25%
       Cancer        10%      air      24%
       Leo           10%
       Virgo          9%
       Libra          7%
       Scorpio        7%
       Sagitarius    10%
       Capricorn      7%
       Aquarius       9%
       Pisces         8%
```

The original Neutrogena Virgo luncheon memo

Must See TV

14. It was my birthday, and I couldn't sleep. I was alone in the Sheraton near the QVC studios in Exton, Pennsylvania, the night before making my first on-air appearance on the TV shopping network. They had told me a Saturday-morning time slot was a good one—millions of people would be sitting on their sofas sipping their second cups of coffee, looking to be dazzled by a new product. So I lay against my headboard in the dark watching the clock, counting down the minutes before I'd be looking into the cameras. *Why did I think this was a good idea?*

∞

Several months earlier, after tossing and turning in my own bed, I stumbled into the family room of the house we rented in Corte Madera, California, and flipped through the channels, looking for distraction. If I couldn't figure out how to get more people to buy holiday gift sets, my life would become a horror show. So watching *The Texas Chainsaw Massacre*—one of only two choices at 2:00 A.M.—hit too close to home. QVC it was.

Sitting at a table with a ruler was a chatty woman measuring amethysts, selling three stacking gemstone rings while I curled up on the sofa chewing my retainer. (I'd been grinding my teeth to stubs.) I liked this lady Jane. She was talking to *me*. "C'mon, Leslie, look how sparkly! It's only three easy payments of $11.66." Plus shipping and handling. I called the QVC 800 number from our cordless phone, placed my order, and went back to bed.

After more late nights with my new buddy, Jane, I had a crazy thought: What if *I* went on QVC with bareMinerals? We had launched this innovative formula in our boutiques a year earlier, but it was basically collecting dust; a light foundation in loose powder form that had only five ingredients, at a time when everyone used liquid foundation and no one cared what was in their makeup, was not what women wanted. To educate women, the normal route would have been print ads. But we didn't have the money. I sent in an application to appear on QVC.

They invited me to Pennsylvania for an interview.

I walked in wearing my white bebe pantsuit with the new $30 five-carat QVC cubic zirconia ring I had bought for the occasion. I wanted to look the part: I couldn't pay a celebrity to be the spokesperson, so the spokesperson would be me. The buyer said she would give me a chance and told me the way things worked: Whatever didn't sell would be shipped back. In other words, if this failed, we'd be screwed.

I didn't tell her I was an introvert. I didn't tell her I HATED public speaking*—much less speaking to the NATION. I didn't tell *anyone* that their colleague/friend/wife/mother was risking her company by going on national television. I already knew this was a crazy idea.

And no one had a better idea. Including me.

∞

Thirty seconds till airtime, I was standing next to my host, Lisa Robertson, hoping the mic didn't pick up my heartbeat. I was pretty sure she had no idea how terrified I felt, and I wanted to keep it that way. I prefer not to fail in public, and passion

* *See Nº81. Risk Taking for the Fearful.*

can make you look confident—even when you're taking the biggest risk of your life. Apart from the people in the television studio, nobody even knew I was there. So if I bombed, my plan was to pretend it hadn't happened.

And there was a good chance I would bomb: How do you sell a foundation on TV when women need to match it to their skin tone in person? How do you convince women that changing their makeup routine is a good idea to begin with? *Why did I think this was a good idea?* I lowered my expectations and hoped only that I could tell women I believed in our product—without throwing up on national television.

And then . . . I was on. Paralyzed with fear. Not wanting to be there. Which is the nature of risk: Risk makes you afraid. You don't get to choose whether or not to be afraid. Only whether to dive in, despite your fear. If you wait for the fear to go away, the opportunity will go away too. I wanted the opportunity.

I asked viewers to imagine a makeup that was good for their skin, a healthy alternative to the liquid they were using.

The phones in the studio started ringing.

Six minutes later, the SOLD OUT graphic flashed on the studio monitor and on TV screens across the country.

And I was literally tingling, head to toe. It didn't feel as amazing as the day my son was born. But it was up there. It changed my life.

But what happened *next* is what changed everything.

Trust the River

15. Sitting in my office in San Francisco, I heard a shout over the cubicle from the customer service department.* Maureen, a QVC viewer from Georgia, had called to find out what nail polish I'd been wearing for those six minutes on TV. I snatched the phone from the gal sitting next to me, and Maureen and I ended up talking for an hour. Maureen told me about the QVC message boards, where women were buzzing with a million questions about bareMinerals. So that night I went online—and I didn't leave for ten years.

Online hangouts were fairly new in the late 1990s, and the moment I joined in, I was instantly reminded of how much I'd missed just blabbing with people about my day. I'd been so consumed with work and family that I barely took time to talk to my next-door neighbor. And many others felt the same way: Debbe from Minnesota was in it, Kesha from Alaska was in it, Christa from Georgia was in it, I was in it. Long after our families were in bed, we were at our desktop computers, typing. We talked about buffing with the right complexion brush, about our kids' favorite movies, Super Bowl

---

* *There were seven of us. The customer service department was whoever answered the phone.*

dip recipes, and right back to concealing rosacea . . . opening up about our personal lives, sometimes talking about makeup. The online connectivity was effortless, electric—and *magnetic*.

People would find us, we would welcome them in, and they would grab their friends to widen the circle. In between my QVC shows, even more people would discover our community. As the community grew, I enlisted my team to come into the mix. With more people came more questions and more energy. It was a rush with no limit, like being on the rapids in a raft with everyone we knew. The energy was high, the pace was fast, and we didn't have time to overthink it.

We trusted the river to take us on the ride of our lives, safe in one another's company. There was no business plan. Not a whiteboard in sight. Only white water—a living, breathing force of nature. Human nature. The *humanest* of nature . . . and there was no denying the power of the current. The only choice we made was to go with the flow—in collaboration, in service, in gratitude, in the moment. We were fully in the present, and we didn't realize we were creating the future.

Me, taking calls

Count Your Lucky Pennies

16. My dad gave me the nickname "Eagle Eye" for my lucky-penny spotting as a kid. So, naturally, I believed I was lucky. Good things kept happening to me. Mostly because I was not paying as much attention to the bad things. When I broke both wrists at the same time when I was thirteen (playing football), I said I was lucky it wasn't worse.

Years later, my husband, Keith, said we needed to do something about my overflowing collection of pennies. We packed them into the back of our Volvo station wagon (all eight thousand of them), and I brought them to the Bare warehouse, where we carefully placed every one into a lip-gloss kit we called "Change Is Good." Why not spread the luck? We sold out.

If you're not already catching on, the secret is: I *choose* to be lucky. This is the best trick you can play on yourself. It's like magic. I've been saying I am lucky for so many decades now that my luck has taken on an almost mystical quality. Really. I win raffles. All the time.

So, right here, right now, I am giving you a tip that can change your life:

Step №1 (there is only one step): Tell yourself and others you are a lucky person. Do that and you will become one.

If you are a parent tell your kids early on that they're lucky. Will shit* happen? Sure, maybe, I don't know. But maybe you and your kids will pay more attention to the lucky stuff.**

---

* *I tried really hard to keep the language clean. Couldn't do it.*

** *The other day someone told me that putting shoes on your bed was bad luck and I said, "It's only bad luck if you believe in that shit."*

Don't Worry, Mom & Dad

17. I've been reading my diaries from my high school days. Let me take that back. I've been *trying* to read my diaries from high school—and I can't. It is excruciating. I am beside myself with embarrassment, and I am the only one who has ever read them. Not one glimmer of youthful wisdom. Empty. Trivial. Gibberish. Basically, I just gushed about boys and how I looked in outfits.

If there's anything good to come from the mortification I am now feeling, here it is: Moms and dads, when you are worried sick that your kid will grow up to be self-absorbed and never amount to anything, don't worry (too much).

I'm OK. They're OK.

Here is a glimpse of entries from my diary.

June 19, 1975

Dear Diary,

Dore and MaryAnn had a pool party with the boys. We kissed. It was super duper.

Dear Diary,

This year was pretty good. Not the best. Oh, by the way, I read all my old diaries. I am going to miss everybody in this diary. I guess this year a lot of bad things happened and some good things. I hope 1976 is a much better year. Suzanne and Regina are my good friends. Jackie and her so-called gang act like cool shit. I hope her hair falls out. But that is my opinion now. My grades were pretty good.

Don't Be a Copycat

18. My mother wouldn't let me buy platform shoes (with her money), so I wrote to my grandparents. Here's their response:

> *April 20, 1975:*
>
> *About the platform shoes, I think your mother knows more than you do, and I agree with her. You probably like them because other girls wear them. Don't be a copycat. They are no good for your feet.*
>
> *This is all for now.*
>
> *Lots of love and kisses to you from Grandpa and Grandma*

Between my grandparents and my mother, I wasn't allowed to look like the other girls. Which was fine, because I rarely did. My mother made my clothes, just like her mother had made her clothes.

I don't sew, but I got the message loud and clear. I learned how to put my own spin on things. You have to actively fight the urge to be the same as everybody else. Use your feet to lead, not follow.

Think a
Few
Steps Ahead
(Good Feet
Are
Important
Later in Life)

19.

Another important missive on the topic of platform shoes:

April 20, 1975:

Dear Leslie,

We are very proud of you. Just do your best, and you will always be on top. About the platform shoes, just forget about them. You are a tall girl, and you don't need elevation. Believe me, Leslie, they ruin your feet, and good feet are important in your later life. Who even wants clumsy feet? And they are so ugly looking. I know you are very sensible and don't want to look cheap.

With love,
Your grandma

Eventually I bought myself the platform shoes (with my own money). Here I am, forty-two years later, and my feet are killing me.

Make Something Out of Nothing

20. Picking pine cones was easy and free as long as we didn't get caught. Mom would drive off the highway at 65 miles per hour and park our Ford station wagon behind a grove of pine trees. Our job was to twist off and grab the pine cones. Quickly. When our bags were full, we'd hop into the car as Mom revved the engine, and we would speed off. Safely home, we'd play show tunes on the turntable as we made pine cone Christmas wreaths with red velvet bows that we could sell for $25 a pop.

When I wasn't performing highway robbery with Mom, I carved sculptures out of Ivory soap, wove floral crowns out of dandelions, and twisted cocktail rings out of colored telephone wire. Don't even get me started on Popsicle sticks, string, and shoeboxes.

Making stuff makes me feel like an artist. This has nothing to do with talent. Shaping and tinkering with your hands has been proven to strengthen the connection between your left and right brain, which helps you visualize creative solutions to life's other puzzles. Also, if you're stuck on a problem over here, and you make something over there, it clears out the blockage. It gets you off your phone, and your finished products make great talking points. Like my Bob Dylan needlepoint pillow.

If you don't know where to start, don't worry. You have a load of ingredients right under your nose—sticky notes, highlighters, a stapler—and you will get better quickly.

Use your hands, not just your thumbs.

The
Power of
Being
Ordinary

21. If you've never heard of Ziggy, he was a comic strip character created by Tom Wilson. Ziggy was an average guy with no hair, no pants, and quite possibly no teeth—he rarely smiled, so you never knew. But he made me smile—and sigh. I wanted to give him a hug, because he made me never feel alone in my weird insecurities. And he was self-reliant and clever—I mean, he asked another comic strip for psychiatric advice! Most of all, he was chill: He never tried to prove anything or best anyone, he didn't make a mountain out of a molehill, and if things went wrong, he carried on. The guy just had a good attitude about life, and, most of all, he was humble.

I miss Ziggy. In a world where aspirational quotes are everywhere, including on coffee mugs and doormats that tell us, "Shoot for the moon. Even if you miss, you'll land among the stars," I find myself wondering why those same words sometimes fall flat for me. *Why don't I buy into this stuff?* Instead, I find myself feeling alive in the power of being ordinary, going through the same things as everyone else. I don't need to reach for the stars today. I just need to plug in the coffee maker to feel like I made it.

Real Friendships Are Good Business

22. Lisa Robertson, the blindingly beautiful, brilliant, and devoted professional that she was, hosted most of my shows. Boy, did she take her position seriously. She lived it, and viewers adored her for it.

We became fast friends. Like, real friends. She invited me to stay at her house whenever I was scheduled to do a show. She called her guest room *my* room. She gave me soft sheets and a duvet (I had never heard of a duvet before). She made me pancakes at 2:00 A.M.; she sang me show tunes in her car. We snacked on her special spicy popcorn while we watched old movies and sat on her closet floor while I admired her shoe collection.

It was those balmy summer nights that I remember most, though. We would pull up in her car near a grassy patch in West Chester, Pennsylvania, and turn off the headlights. We would sit in silence and watch the fireflies perform a light show to rival the Fourth of July.

When we were on air together, our friendship took on a new dimension that only amplified the relationship we had together off the air. Our viewers were drawn to our bond, and our chemistry was contagious. We told stories, laughed until our ribs hurt, and sold a ton of makeup.

People want to belong to something real. You can't *ideate* a friendship. And it turns out, genuine friendships can be good business too.

Lisa and me on our day off

You Owe It to Your Co-workers Not to Be Boring

23. Ever wish you could live without food? Or water? Or sleep? Allowing you to be the first one into work and the last one out, because you are always at your desk, twenty-four hours a day, seven days a week, outworking everyone, for the rest of your life, which never ends, because this is hell?

Be careful what you wish for.

All that working at work makes it hard to work on *yourself*. Read a book. Take an improv class. Learn to play the harmonica. A great company has great people. Great people cultivate themselves.

Get a life, and bring it to work.

Giving Is the Gift That Keeps On Giving

24. When Keith started noticing that things were missing from the shelves in the family room—things he thought belonged to him—I told him the truth: Women in our online community were taking our stuff, because I was giving it away—and not just the hand-carved cameos we'd picked up on vacation in Italy. Anyone wear size 9.5 pumps? Need a leather handbag? How about my lucky-penny collection?*

* See Nº16. Count Your Lucky Pennies.

I have always loved giving gifts to friends. So giving gifts to people who loved our products just felt right. Because it brought us closer together.

My favorite gift was the red dress, an evening gown I wore one night on QVC for a charity auction to benefit Cancer and Careers. Seven women were bidding on it at the same time—and at the last minute an eighth woman swooped in with the winning bid.

A year later, a package showed up in the mail: Inside was the gown and a handmade book. It was called *The Adventures of the Traveling Red Dress*, and it told the story through words and photographs of how all eight women had shared the dress, mailing it from one to another, and how they had felt when they wore it—deeply personal stories about their lives and dreams.

It blew me away. And it made me feel EXACTLY as I'd hoped others would feel when I gave gifts to them: thrilled . . . connected . . . *intimate*. We had all worn the same dress.

Keith, to his credit, understood.* He started hiding stuff he didn't want to disappear. A good marriage is like a good business that way: They both run on mutual respect. Especially when you bring your values to work—and you bring your work home.

Humans Have Needs

---

25. Generally speaking, it's not a good idea to invite a bunch of people you've never met to your hotel room.

But we were corresponding online for months (this was on the Bare chat rooms in 1999, not on Tinder today), and we agreed the internet wasn't cutting it. Not a surprise, because people have physical bodies, and they like to be physical with them. (Probably why Tinder took off too.) So

I messaged the chat rooms with an idea for an in-person get-together after the next QVC show.

When the cameras turned off, everyone in the live studio audience piled into their cars and followed me back to my room at the Sheraton for a pizza party. Women packed into the suite, sat on the floor, on the bed, on the windowsill, scarfing slices and playing makeup. It felt like we were back in high school—only we were grown-ups with kids back at home. This was just the start.

Before long, I was flying to Vegas to go to a show with a group of customers who wanted to make a weekend getaway out of it. I joined women on "customer cruises." While our competitors were buying print ads in glossy magazines, we were putting our marketing dollars to work renting Lady Gaga's bus to tour the country, stopping in shopping malls, random parking lots, and people's houses along the way.

Why is this important? Because if there is anything I've learned from being a part of a growing community, it's this:

Communities are made of people. People are human. Humans have physical needs.

Make
Your
Walls
Talk

26. I had a massive wall in the hallway outside my office. It became an art installation that had a life of its own. It told hundreds of stories. Visitors would stop by, and new hires would spend time poking around, finding small treasures.

The wall was an ever-evolving collection of letters, photos, and artwork from our customers. Visual storytelling. Nonfiction. Poems and feathers. We would cram on as many items as we could, and the thing actually came to life. It was full of perspectives and ideas we hadn't thought of. An eyeshadow worn as a lip balm? Read about it on the wall. A thank-you note to one of our beauty ambassadors for making a house call? Read about it on the wall. A toddler sitting on the toilet reading a bareMinerals catalog? Just plain cute.

You could touch the wall, and it would touch you back.

Go find a wall. Bring it to life. Seeing is believing.

Letter Writing as a Policy

27. I like people more than numbers. In business, people often become numbers. Order number, credit card number, and my favorite, a statistic. I always find that when people inside the company know real customers' names, they instantly have more empathy. They automatically care.

Which is why we had letter writing as a policy.

When you joined our company, you had to send a handwritten note to a customer from our database with a personal anecdote revealing something about yourself. Companies already know a ton about the people using their products, yet customers usually know nothing about the people making them. Turnabout was only fair.

This is far from a dumb idea. It has the potential to knock someone's socks off, and it's unexpected for both parties—the one asked to write the note and the one receiving it. Some people even received letters back from the customers. Human contact makes us humans together.

It's the write thing to do.*

* *My editor REALLY wanted me to take this line out.*

Your Customers Are a Lot Smarter Than You

-----

28. I hung on to every word as she gave me the pep talk of my life. This was the time I called her for her counsel on a speech I was writing for a beauty industry conference. Per usual, her sage words calmed my nerves as she guided me out of the weeds and back to the roots of what we were really doing as a business. "Your business paradigm hinges on two things—that of creating relationships between the company and the clients and the clients creating relationships with one another."

She was talking about how it wasn't just about building relationships between the company and the customer but that the women in the community ended up creating deep bonds with *one another*. Good point, and it was true. All that connectivity led to new products and even our philanthropic program, which was developed by the community from beginning to end with Terry's guidance.

Terry Ross was my trusted advisor. But before that, she was a customer I'd met in the online chat room that she co-hosted. She was wicked smart, with piercing insights, and I wanted to be like her someday.

"How do you do it?" I wanted to know.

"I'm from the South," she told me.

Terry is a stay-at-home mother who lives in a small town in Michigan with her husband and three kids, the ultimate bareMinerals advocate, natural leader, and knitter extraordinaire. She had a lot of opinions about how to grow the community, and we listened. Her candid wisdom was liberally distributed to the global teams and to investors and was used in onboarding materials.

I spent the early part of my career working at large companies where there were bottomless spreadsheets, but not once had I asked a living customer for advice. When your customers care as much as you do about bringing standout experiences to the world, you can learn a ton from them.

Just as Terry once said, "You bring the reality of the human condition into your business; if you continue to do that, you will never go wrong."

Nighttime Ritual

29. There's something about the nighttime that gives those nasty voices in my head a little too much airtime. Years ago, it felt like they were taping their own podcast, called *Reasons Why Leslie Is Such a Failure.*

After a while, I could see it coming, and before I sank into the abyss, I would reach under my nightstand and pull out my Bedside Reading file.

The file (technically a binder) was stuffed with uplifting missives from customers and colleagues—letters, emails, and even napkins with scribbles. I saved anything that would get me in true form for the next morning.

The file was my express ticket to greater perspective. Every note I read was a reminder that people counted on us, and I counted on them. Like the story from a girl with acne who finally felt confident enough to look people in the eye, or the one about Caroline, a high school student from Norway who moved to Sacramento for a year to live with a mom she knew from the bareMinerals online community, even though they had never met in person. Or the handwritten letter from Pete Born, the legendary journalist and heart and soul of the beauty industry, whose kindness continues to blow me away. And that's the point. Kind words from people you admire and respect will always overcome that day's trials.

Why not give it a shot?

1. Collect reminders that lift you above the fray.
2. Write kind notes for someone else's file.
3. Take back the night.

Knock
Each
Other
Out

30. Coming up with dull ideas is as easy as baking a vanilla cake: Just follow the recipe for the same result every time. There is no recipe for sharp ideas, however. Sharp ideas are unpredictable.

So we introduced unpredictability into our brainstorming process. To warm up before creative meetings, we always started with a few push-ups or jogging in place to get the blood going. Then we filled up with our fuel of choice: caffeine.

THEN came a surprise move. Mine might be to ask everyone how they'd chosen their outfit that day. Or to tell their life story in six words. Didn't matter what I did, except that it was spontaneous and unexpected, which gets people lighter on their toes and feeling more energetic. As energy levels increased, ideas would start to bounce. The bouncing created a rhythm. And then sometimes . . . a thud. The good kind: One of us (me) would laugh* so hard, she'd fall out of her swivel chair, land on the floor, and stay there.

Because this is where I wanted us to be: open to the moment, open to one another, tossing around ideas in a natural flow—until things started to land, and we finally knocked each other out with a Great Idea.

See Nº54. Leading with Laughter.

Keep Your Pants On

31. When I asked the VP of Product Development to come into my office and take off her pants, it seemed like a good idea. I had lost a few pounds. I loved her jeans. And I thought it would be cool to see if they fit me.

It's not like I didn't know her. I had asked her to the house a few times to watch Trent. So trying on her pants seemed like the next step in our relationship. Which is why it felt only mildly weird to see her taking off her pants in the middle of my office.

Until I took off *my* pants, and it hit me: *This is REALLY weird. Leslie, what were you thinking?*

OK, I still tried on her jeans.

I am horrified telling you this. This was *not* cool. It was a massive mistake. But I've decided not to *regret* it, because I gave up regret. This is an important distinction.

Regret is something you carry in your pocket—like a set of keys that weighs ten pounds. Or a tattoo that says, *Rigret.* So you feel stupid, along with sad and remorseful, for the rest of your life.

Versus acknowledging a *mistake,* which is something to remember only so you don't repeat it. And, truly, how could you have lived your life without making mistakes? Relationship mistakes. Career mistakes. Parenting mistakes. The list goes on, the older you get.

Which set me to investigate, what do older people regret before they die? Worrying too much.

It would be a REAL mistake not to remember *that.*

Fine print: Sarina and I are friends to this day—and she approved this content.

Find Yourself a Pen Pal

32. Andrew Rodgers lives in London, looks like a movie star, and spent his career in the beauty industry. He is now my pen pal.

Not that looks matter. When your relationship is epistolary, what's inside is what counts: Are you interesting? Are you *interested*?

Andrew is both, and I don't say that lightly. I am to pen pals what Cleopatra was to lovers: I've had a few.

At one point, I had ten pen pals *at the same time*—from Peru, Germany, Australia, and Finland. This was back in fifth grade, when our teacher paired us with kids from around the world, and

I discovered not only was their handwriting better than mine, so was their English. I loved getting their letters in the mail. Which has inspired me ever since to write cards, letters, and notes— because you have to give to get.

About five years ago, I decided to find someone who appreciated the lost art of exchanging letters. Someone willing to skip the chitchat and see what we could discover about each other and ourselves. A true pen pal.

I had some rules:

- Handwritten correspondence only
- No fewer than three pages per missive
- No emailing in between letters except to ask if the letter has been received
- For Your Eyes Only, so get personal. (If it isn't personal, you are wasting a perfectly good John Lennon stamp.)

I had known Andrew professionally for many years. But we were not besties. We just had mutual respect. So I asked him if he was up for taking the challenge.

Given our rules, all I can tell you is, this guy can write! Which inspires me to write. Which makes me feel (if not look) like a movie star—or actually, like one of my rock stars: Ben Franklin— because he wrote a lot of letters.

Write Me

33. Sometimes it takes one letter to get into the swing of things. It's about making the time and finding cool stamps. If you really can't find someone to write to, write me, and I will write back. I also use goofy stickers.

Here's my P.O. Box:

Leslie Blodgett
1 Blackfield Drive
P.O. Box 329
Tiburon, CA 94920

Fine print: If you plan to take me up on this offer, you'd better tell me something juicy about yourself. It will be our little secret.

Plan to Be Spontaneous

34. I was standing onstage looking out at a sea of men in suits looking up at me. *Nightmare.* Did I mention I hate public speaking?* These guys (and most of them were guys) were investors in the private equity fund that had invested in our company, and I was about to present the bareMinerals story. I had heard about "pedigrees" when talking about dogs but never about people: yet the guy who just presented had a slide of all his advanced degrees, and I didn't have even a business degree (still don't)—but I did use more than twenty products on my face.

So that's how I decided to introduce myself, as I stood before the mic: "I may not have a Harvard MBA, but I do have eleven pounds of makeup upstairs in my hotel room." And just like that, my risky, *unplanned* confession broke the ice into a million sparkly pebbles and gave me cred without the (student loan) debt.

As a rule, I didn't go to many of these conferences, because I preferred growing the business—and not speaking in public. But whenever I did have to speak, I applied the lesson I learned that day in the grand ballroom of the fancy Boston hotel: Always plan to be spontaneous. I do love eliminating any chance of crashing and burning onstage as much as the next glossophobe.* But when you need to ease the tension with an audience (and within yourself), nothing works better than reading the room and speaking your mind. For about four seconds, if you're me. Then it's back to the script. A little riffing goes a long way.

* *See Nº81. Risk Taking for the Fearful.*

As Long as You Are Wearing Clothes...

35. Why not use them?
    Some people talk about power
clothes: wardrobe choices that give you a surge of
confidence in a meeting, on a date, in an interview.
I don't necessarily wear power clothes, but I am
a big fan of *using* my clothes to speak for me—
sometimes even literally. Like my necklace that
says *LOVE* in huge letters, or the *I Really Like You*
T-shirt I most recently sported to an appointment
with my new gynecologist. Even if your clothes
don't literally spell out words to someone else, you
can use them as little reminders to yourself.
    Some of my favorites:

- *Keep your promises* T-shirt under my jacket
  at a business meeting
- A blouse with a ruffle down the front to
  remind me not to ruffle feathers
- A safari-style jacket to tell myself that
  the people I was presenting to were just a
  bunch of animals and that they wouldn't
  intimidate me
- Tiaras. Let's just say I own more than one,
  and they have myriad applications.

Bring Your Life to Work

36. My son didn't rake leaves growing up, because we didn't have leaves. But he did have a Madagascar chameleon named Zeppo, so he created an eye shadow collection based on Zeppo's colors.

I realize creating eye shadows inspired by a Madagascar chameleon isn't for everyone. But if you work, you likely have a place of work. And you can bring your kid to that place and let him (or her) poke around.

In my case, Trent came to the office, he joined me on trips to the mall to visit boutiques, he came to my speaking gigs, and he even joined me on QVC. He watched. He listened. He learned what I was up to. Then he mixed it all up for himself in an idea for eye shadows.

Today, sweet Zeppo is gone. (He spent his last days in a cage in Trent's bedroom, hanging upside down from a tree branch, before climbing into his final resting place: the cardboard coffin custom-made by Keith. Now *that* is a handy man!) But Zeppo's legacy lives on, in more ways than one.

Making eye shadows means mixing loose minerals and putting them in jars. Trent's company is called Spice Tribe, which blends loose spices and packages them in jars.

Coincidence?

Be Pen Pals with Your Kid

37. Being a working mother filled me with love—and, sometimes, *envy*.

I had the career, so it made sense for Keith to stay home and raise Trent—and go to the Little League games and the school activities and the birthday parties—while I flew around the country (and sometimes the world) and then back home, where I'd hear about their great times together while I packed for the next trip. Which led to fantasies of Trent clutching my leg and begging me not to leave as I stood by the door with my suitcase.

Versus the reality of him once telling me, after I asked him if he wanted me to quit my job, "No, Mom, we're good." Evidently only one of us felt disconnected from the family unit.

That's why I forced my son to be my pen pal. I figured, if this kid has the nerve to be perfectly happy without me around, the least he can do is write to me about it! And maybe—just maybe—he will find the idea of reading secret letters from his mom kind of cool. Maybe to the point of waiting on the curb for the mailman like I did when I was a kid. So that, ultimately, he will miss me! Or at least miss my letters.

There were only two rules: All letters had to be addressed to our home, and we could never speak of them to anyone—not even to each other.

The result: When I saw a letter from Trent waiting on the kitchen table, I would run off to my room, sit on the floor behind the bed, and tear open the letter like I did when I was ten. As for Trent . . . I don't know that he ever waited on the curb for the mailman. He was busy, which sometimes meant he was answering my letters.

And sitting on my bedroom floor, reading letters only I got to read—conversations only we got to have—made me feel like the most special mom in the world—which I thought about a lot on the way back to the airport.

Don't Be a Jerk

38.

Dear Trent,

You may find this hard to believe, coming from your mother, but I have a crazy hyper empathy gene. I am driven to help others—OK, mainly other women. But I like to think that I helped you find your way, even when I was out of the house supporting our family by trying to help women.

So it came as something of a shock to me when I found myself tempted to be less than helpful to a close childhood friend who accused me of doing a bad job as your mother. Hers was probably the most unusual letter I have ever received in my life. And, as you know from the box of notes from colleagues and clients that I keep by my bedside to read when I want to cheer myself up, I receive a LOT of letters.*

Here's a cut-and-paste of the most powerful paragraph; i.e., the one that inspired me to consider sacrificing the fundamental value on which I

See Nº29. Nighttime Ritual.

built my career—empathy—and giving in to what psychologists call "revenge fantasies."

> *It is selfish for women to leave their children to pursue a career (in the name of "feminism" and "leaning in" and "balance" and whatever words you want to put on it). To have a career gives the children a feeling that they are not as important to their mother as her job is, that her job comes first. That is always wrong, and no matter how well Keith has taken care of Trent, he could never take the place of Trent's mother. Men are men, and women, women. I wouldn't praise the fact that Keith did such a great job so you could leave your motherly responsibilities behind all these years.*

A dear childhood friend . . . a *woman* . . . criticizing me as a businesswoman, a wife, *your mom* . . . trying to tear me down on every level of my life . . . it was painful.

But it did inspire what I thought was a great idea. And as I always do when I think I have a great idea, whether it's for a new product to even out skin tone or a new way to get even, I crowdsourced opinions: I asked a few colleagues to join me in my office, closed the door, and read the letter out loud.

When I finished reading, one colleague said, "What are we gonna do?" Like we were in this together—like family. Another colleague was speechless—which he NEVER is. That's when I shared my great idea: "Let's post her email to my Facebook page!" In other words, *Let's bring her down!* They both agreed, "That's a great idea!"

But, just in case we were wrong, I took another page from my "What I learned about life from my career" book,* and I decided to reflect.

Then I wrote my old friend a card: *Enjoy your gifts.* I put it in a box full of bareMinerals products and dropped the box into the mail. And I felt GREAT—for days.

* *Which is basically what's in this book, plus the boring stuff.*

I bet if psychologists studied situations like this, they'd find that every time we counter a toxic action with a healthy one, we release endorphins—a kind of internal ecstasy that lasts long after the event.

What I'm trying to say is, I LOVE my career, but I truly, madly, deeply love *you* most of all. And even if you didn't understand this growing up, there's something I want you to know now: I think the most important thing any parent can do is walk the talk—actually live the values she wants her son or daughter to live by. So if nothing else, I hope my life stands as an example to be true to yourself.

Throughout your life you will run into people who want to hurt you or put you down or make you angry. You may fantasize about payback. That's your inner jerk tempting you, which is totally normal. Maybe there is the occasional Mother Teresa out there who does not dream of getting even when someone cuts her to the core— but I am Mother Leslie. Revenge sounded good to me—for a moment. But once I settled down and went to that quiet place where I make my best decisions, I was able to resist the temptation to be a jerk and behave in a way that was consistent with my values. And as sweet as revenge might feel, feeling like yourself is the most AWESOME feeling of all.

Love,
Mom

Sometimes It Just Feels Right

39. It was 2009, and the stock market was tanking. So I wrote a full-page ad, and I ran it in the *New York Times*. The economy may have been ugly, but women could still feel healthy and beautiful.

We'd never done anything like this. I hadn't researched circulation or demographics. I wasn't a copywriter. I was just a regular reader of the *New York Times*, and something about it felt right.

The ad was really more like a full-page *letter* to people who maybe hadn't heard of us yet. I wrote it one night in my living room before bed. I had always heard in the advertising world that readers don't like to read a lot of words—so I made that the headline: *The advertising experts tell us that people don't read tons of copy.*

And people did read, right to the end, which was my favorite part of the letter: I invited folks to come in for coffee when they were in San Francisco. I included our receptionist Hilda's phone number and gave her a heads-up the night before.*

Hilda's phone rang a lot over the next week. We got calls from people wondering if we were for real. Calls to tell us we were cool. Even a call from a journalist to say my grammar was terrible.

OK, so this was not a page ripped from a business book. But if you find yourself at the Starbucks on the corner picking up trays of lattes for complete strangers who want to visit your office, you know what you're doing makes sense.

---

* *Hilda and I had met years before at the hair salon where we were both clients. I had foils in my hair, and she told me to hold on for ten minutes while she raced home to bring in her makeup to show me. I hired her on the spot.*

The
Jay Effect

---

40. Around the time we were going to
launch our first liquid foundation,
Luawanna, a loyal customer from Sun Valley,
Idaho, heard the buzz and felt compelled to email
me about a heated debate she and her husband,
Jay, had had over dinner. Jay's opinion was that
our entire business had been built on the original
foundation in a loose powder form and that

we were selling out by launching a new liquid foundation that went against the company values. One of the reasons behind the new launch was that women were telling us they wanted a liquid made with our rigorous product development principles. We agreed. We wanted all women to have the opportunity to use our products. Luawanna understood our decision and had already preordered the new foundation in four shades.

What do you do with this information?

1. My God, celebrate that this married couple was having a (heated) discussion about your brand over dinner.
2. Ask yourself: Is Jay saying what thousands of people may be thinking?

Jay helped us sharpen our message to the community and the broader public before the actual product launch. He led us to tell the story behind *why* we were doing it and in a way that was respectful to our customers and company philosophy. When a brand starts moving into new territory, it's smart to listen to the periphery.

That's the Jay Effect: listening to all people invested in the brand, not just the obvious ones.

The Stuff Washes Off

41. I am a fan of learning to do makeup early. As a parent you might say, "No way do I want my daughter (or son) wearing makeup at thirteen." OK, how about twelve? For the record, I'm not proposing wearing a cat eye to soccer practice, but getting the basics down allows you to present yourself to the world the way you want the world to see you.

It does take practice:

Wielding a mascara wand is like sword fighting: You want to stay on target, or you will get poked. And be sure to replace your tube before you get the uni-lash. (That's when the formula is so old, it glues your eyelashes together.)

The lone eye shadow is a thing, and I like it for beginners. Nude shades are smart. ("Nude" means any color similar to your skin tone.) A little crystal sheen with the nude is a plus.

People are brow-happy these days. Easy, Tiger. Don't get defined by your brows until you know what you are getting yourself into. Do a little research, and have fun. If people keep asking why you look surprised, try again.

The tip of the eyeliner should be thin and pointed so you can get as close to the lash line as possible. Slow down and use little strokes until you are in control. Some liners are so slippery, they'll glide to your ear. That's a sign you went too far. Try again.

I want to see you, not your foundation. Learn to blend. Cover zits if you wish, but don't conceal freckles ('cause they're awesome).

Play around, learn what works, practice. This goes for any age or ability—and not just for makeup. Experiments are good. This stuff washes off.

Risky
Business

42. For a million years (OK, decades) the best way to build a beauty brand was by using professional models in glossy print ads.

We did the opposite: We got the word out in our own infomercials using real customer stories. We flew our consumers in from all over the country, and we didn't retouch every last bit of humanity out of their faces. The "models" on our website and packaging were people we knew by name: customers, friends, even someone I met at the gym. In fact, our best-selling Get Started Kit featured the face of Andrea Rosenthal, from our training team.

One day, after bareMinerals had become a recognized brand, the team felt it was time to try something new. Which ended up being something radical for us: "Let's go where all of our competition is—in the glossy magazines." Okaaay, I guess. But when it came time to hire models from a two-dimensional collection of flawless photographs, it just felt wrong. How do you make a shift like that without losing the values on which you built the company? We saw beauty in women's stories as well as their faces. What would happen to the story part?

Then somebody at the ad agency had an idea. *What if we did a blind casting?*

We invited a few hundred candidates to fill out a questionnaire, answering questions like: What is your motto? Do you have any pets? And we interviewed our ninety favorites in person. Only we didn't actually *see* any of them—they were on the other side of a partition. We just listened, which is exactly what we had been doing with people from the beginning. Based on those conversations, we chose five women to represent our brand, and we signed them up. *Without ever seeing their faces.* Let that sink in.

It was a huge risk. *What if it completely backfires? What if they all turn out to be twenty-five and blond?* We started to panic and almost pulled the plug at the last minute.

The five women were totally unique, and, even better, we *liked* them as people.

It would have been easy to hire a bunch of pretty faces, and it probably would have worked—on a commercial level. But our approach also worked on an emotional level—it brought everyone together into a shared experience. Our employees and customers got to see that we were still the real thing.

Messing Around with Pot

43. BareMinerals was packaged in jars. A jar is a container, and so is a pot. Pot is also a plant that people use to get high.

We had a little fun with pot once when we were developing a brand awareness campaign. We asked women to *rethink* what they put on their skin, specifically:

RETHINK THE BENEFITS OF A LITTLE POT.

In this case, we were referring to pot, the vessel. We planted this poster about thirty feet from my office, because it made us (me) laugh every time I passed it.

We were already having fun and laughing at work, so we used our advertising to invite our customers in on the joke. And we knew that if we could catch their attention and make them smile, they would feel a connection and remember us.

We never limited ourselves to the obvious places for humor either. We'd slip funny notes inside our packaging and post one-liners to the walls of our boutiques. Where store displays would advertise products for "Creating a smoky eye" or "Concealing dark circles," ours said: "This is our most shoplifted shade."

Recognize the benefits of injecting a little humor into your brand. Connection, surprise, and a good chuckle are all natural side effects. You don't need to smoke anything either.

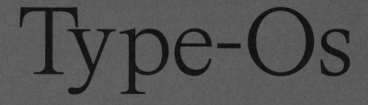

44. Philosophers read novels in their spare time. At least one great novelist studied butterflies. And I like stories about nature and fitness, and I almost never read about beauty.

In other words, it doesn't take an Einstein to realize that whatever your industry, it's a good idea to look somewhere else for new ideas—though Einstein knew this too.* A photo essay about the Great Barrier Reef, for example, gets me thinking about using more sea ingredients; a profile of Guatemalan women weaving their own clothing opens my mind to a new color palette; and an article on the latest camping device that allows you to dangle from the face of a mountain inspires me to take more risks.

The same principle applies to people: when I'm building a team, I don't rely only on professionals who have worked in the same industry their entire careers. I like blending a little fresh blood into the mix: type O, for Original thinkers.

* *"We cannot solve our problems with the same thinking we used when we created them."*

A
Breakfast
Recipe

---

45. I have no business giving cooking tips, but my oatmeal breakfast rocks. I call it Look Fab in Leggings Breakfast. Note: Serving size is pretty key here. Only ⅛ cup of microwavable oats. If you make more, then it's not my recipe, and you are on your own.

In a microwavable bowl, combine:

- ⅛ cup of oatmeal
- A little bit of peanut butter
- Half a banana, sliced thin
- Many, many shakes of cinnamon
- 1 egg white (Don't get weirded out by the egg thing. Think about oatmeal cookies.)
- ¼ cup of water

Place cling wrap over the bowl.

Heat 1 minute 10 seconds in the microwave (or longer—I don't know how well your microwave works).

Stir with spoon.

Taste it with an open mind. It will grow on you.

Notes: The Look Fab in Leggings Breakfast is inspired by a recipe I picked up in a hard-core bodybuilder magazine. It has everything someone needs to feel full and promotes lean body mass. I love the protein (egg) and good fiber (oats), and cinnamon is known to curb appetite. I added the banana, and sometimes I throw in golden raisins. But no more than five.

How to Make a Compelling Introduction

46. When a friend moved her family to New York City, I wanted to introduce her and her husband to another couple. They were all google-able, and I wasn't interested in writing the typical email intro. So I decided to test out a new strategy.

We all have to eat. So I turned my friends into my favorite foods. Here's how my email intro turned out:

Andy = a chocolate chip cookie
You can take him anywhere, and people will thank you for bringing him. Well-loved. Big personality, the right amount of sweet (no gimmicks).

Jessica = your Italian grandma's meatballs (with or without sauce)
Made of the best-quality ingredients, no filler, salt of the earth, soul food on the inside and out. The secret recipe that everyone is trying to get their hands on. And funny. Let's face it, meatballs are funny.

Kurt = key lime pie from the Florida Keys
Smooth, creamy, velvety, and then BAM! That zing takes you by surprise, like, "Where did that come from?" Refreshingly honest. And the crust is the best part.

Tony = a bowl of shishito peppers blistered on the stove top with chunky salt
Spicy, surprising, a little intimidating. Hot stuff, and you never know what you are going to get with this risk-taker. But you have to indulge, or you won't know what you are missing.

The dinner party was a hit. We had pizza.

Get a Sparring Partner

47. Sometimes you get an idea, and you can't get it out of your head.

Maybe it's a product idea. That shower cap you've been thinking about? Been nagging you for years. What if you put a tassel on top that magnetically communicates with your plumbing and adjusts the water pressure throughout the duration of the shower? You *know* it can make an impact—not only because it is fashion-forward but because it can also preserve water.

Great idea, but you never share it. You think maybe you should forget about it. You are pretty good at talking yourself out of your dreams.

You need a sparring partner. Someone* you can count on to tell you that your idea is worthless, pointless, and vain. Why? Because you'll see how good you are at defending it. If you are willing to fight for it, you may finally be spurred to take action—and prove them wrong.

So, find that special someone who gets your goat, and see how your pitch comes to life.

* *Blowhards are best.*

iNap.
And
You
Should
Too.

48. Seven- and eight-year-olds get it right. According to the National Sleep Foundation, they need ten to eleven hours of sleep, and they get it. This makes sense; they don't have a mortgage to worry about. Sleep is important. If you don't get eight hours of sleep, you might die. Not to be morbid—you might die anyway, but not sleeping isn't helping your odds.

My secret to getting some sleep and increasing longevity? Naps.

There are two camps: people who nap and people who wouldn't dare. Most of the non-nappers have an outdated outlook. I'm not talking a two-hour siesta here. Ten minutes.* It's the novella of naps versus the unabridged version.

One power nap a day can save your life. Before I had a sofa in my office, I slept under my desk in case my assistant, Marlene, walked in without knocking. I set the alarm for ten minutes, popped up like a prairie dog when it rang, and scampered off to my next meeting reinvigorated.

* Some experts even suggest having coffee before the nap, since the caffeine takes ten minutes to kick in.

Mind
Your
Muscles

---

49. I was a competitive arm wrestler for a while, and my winningest day was beating six guys in a row at a pizza parlor in San Francisco.* It was so exhilarating that I did a victory lap with a jar of chili flakes raised high in my right hand like a torch.

* *Trent's fourth-grade buddies were strong—but I was stronger.*

Throughout my life, exercising my physical muscles has given me strength that's mostly psychological (although it doesn't hurt that I can also throw my carry-on bags into the overhead compartment with the accuracy of a baseball pitching machine). When I am physically strong, that strength also travels north to my brain, and I am more inclined to tackle, crush, and conquer the larger life hurdles in my path—like people who attempt to cut me in line for a hot dog at a Giants game. (Don't even try.)

So I keep up a modest exercise routine to maintain my muscles, because the health benefits are too massive to ignore, and sometimes it's my *mind* that needs the boost. Over the years I have enjoyed a good workout DVD at home, like P90X or just twenty push-ups on any flat surface,** and for the last nine years I have become a huge barre workout devotee.***

Mind your muscles. Even if you can't see them, it's about knowing they're there to support you in your hour of need.

** *Once, when I met the staff at our boutique at the Mall of America, I gave 'em ten on the mall floor before saying hello. Outside the shop entrance. In a jungle-print jersey dress.*

*** *The Dailey Method and Physique 57 are my scene. (This is not an ad.)*

Leave Yourself Behind

50.

Self-care comes in many forms.

We all love a good massage.

But running to the rescue of a friend is like
shiatsu for the soul.

And I can see in my friends' faces, they feel
that way too

when they help me.

Be kind to yourself by being kind to
someone else.

Take some time away

to leave yourself behind.*

* Coming soon, my book of poetry. Just kidding.

Popcorn Break

51. I postponed my mammogram, again. I forgot to pay my Xfinity bill, and they turned off my service. My car is so dirty, Keith won't get in. And my kid gave me yet another Thich Nhat Hanh book, because he thinks I'm too intense.

So as we reach the midpoint in this book of advice, I thought it would be a good time to remind each other:

1. Be honest with yourself. It's impossible to have meaningful relationships with others if this one's out of whack.
2. We all have fears, foibles, weaknesses. They are what connect us: All of us are flawed.
3. People who *know* they are flawed can give you pretty good advice. By being in touch with their weaknesses, they can help you connect with yours.

In other words, if ever you are tempted to think my life is humming, picture me alone in my dirty car, parked on the side of the road, yelling in frustration because the meditation app stopped streaming.

Namaste.

Onward.

Bloom Your Own Way

52. Imagine being a bush, or a stalk, at the first spring bloom. And instead of petals, you have pods that look like caterpillars. Kids think you are an animal, not a plant. You look strange, but you feel familiar and warm, because you are furry and fuzzy. People touch you, even though you are twiggy. You are cozy, mysterious, curious, and bare. It is perfectly natural to be both humble and bold.

The pussy willow has an edge.

Defy assumptions.

Take
Calls

53. As CEO, I took calls. We were in the same building as the customer service team. Marlene, my assistant, would give me a list of twenty-five people every week. I would call them out of the blue. I'd ask them about their favorite product. How they spent their day. If they had any advice for me. We would just talk.

Sometimes I would ask one of our representatives if I could jump onto their call. Sometimes I would go onto the company Facebook page and give my email address and ask for phone numbers. Sometimes I would even give out my cell phone number (not recommended).

Make making calls a habit, and it soon becomes natural. Like dancing in the hallway between meetings. And if you are thinking you won't hear the truth, you are wrong. I learned way more from giving my number to customers—even the haters we had on social media—than I ever did from any focus groups. Just be normal, and don't force it.

This may seem like a great idea when the company is small and like a distraction when the company grows up. It's not. Don't forget your phone is a phone. Hop on it. Talking to customers is never a distraction. Make time.

Lead with Laughter

54. As it turns out, I have a very loud and somewhat grating laugh. Some people don't like it, but I refuse to tone it down, because a hearty laugh feels great, and nothing good comes from stifling one—and because humorless people are no fun.

If this happens to be the first page you flipped to in this book, welcome to my book, and please note that I am an introvert and I'm not funny. This is key, because neither of these facts has anything to do with bringing a humor mind-set to work.

We were far from a loosey-goosey operation at bare. We were always serious about becoming a leader in the beauty industry. But without levity, we would've fallen short. A culture of humor brought the teams closer together, amped creativity and trust, and took the pressure off. Most important, people brought their whole selves to work, not just the image of the perfectly coiffed professional.

Try on these techniques:

Practice being yourself.
Finding your humor at work is not an invention— it's a rediscovery. Unless you are an inherently sinister human being, your natural style for lightness should be welcomed at work. I liked running around the office barefoot and doing yoga on the conference room table. This may not fly in your space, but you know what will. We all have an innate playful side; dust it off.

Go around the room with an offbeat question.
I would invite employees to my house for cocktail parties, and the best part was mining for untold stories. It was casual and conversational, so everyone was open to participating. It was always funny.

Have a 2:00 P.M. call to action.
At bare everyone would report to the lobby without shoes at 2:00 P.M. We'd dance to two songs and then go back to work. No announcements; we just needed to loosen up and lighten up.

Own Up
and
Own
the Room

55.

The beauty industry is a lot like the panda mating ritual: The male stomps on the female while she plays dead. A simile I once shared with a roomful of beauty professionals to break the ice. Which bombed. For reasons that remain mysterious; I still don't know why this didn't work.

But I owned it, which *always* works. Because being vulnerable gets an audience on your side. Everyone's afraid of something, and most people are afraid to admit it. When you own up, you own the room.

Never Get Jaded

56. We hit the big time: Our brand was a blue square on *Jeopardy!*—the only game show that mattered. This was seriously cool, and we pinched ourselves.

But the second time we made it onto *Jeopardy!* was even better: not only did the contestant get it right, but the contestant was *a dude*. A dude who knew his makeup. I loved him.

It would've made perfect sense to send another cheerful announcement in the weekly newsletter, but that seemed like a measly way to mark this momentous occasion. So after a glass of champagne to celebrate, I texted Alison Reid, our SVP of Brand, to share the news.

AR: "Holy sh*t."

LB: "We gotta find this guy."

AR: "On it."

We found him in Kansas relaxing at home with his wife. On the call, I was getting the impression that my profusive thank-yous may have set off his *Is she nuts?* alarm bells, but he allowed me to continue the interrogation. "Did you win anything?" "Does your wife wear our makeup?" "Do you watch *Game of Thrones*?" And, because who doesn't want under-eye concealer, we followed up with a gift package of bareMinerals.

Which was also a gift to *ourselves*, to celebrate what mattered. We were featured on the only game show that mattered—twice!—*because* of people like the dude who knew his makeup. The dude knew our name. The least we could do was show him we knew his.

Because if you think you're too big to remember who you serve, you're gonna get small, fast. Being successful is never about you. It's about what you do for others. So when someone rewards your service, always, always say thank you.

Real Community Isn't About Followers

57. As a kid, the only time I heard the word "community" was when my town was having a pancake breakfast. For a long time it conjured up bacon and maple syrup. The word is old and comes from the Latin *communis*, which translates very simply to "common, public, shared by many." When I think about the bareMinerals community, this makes sense. The very nature of these relationships was close. Like family. It wasn't us and them. It was just US.

The steady stream of ideas coming in from our customers made for an average day at the office.

They became like our own product development team of scientists and artists creating special blends in their home laboratories (their bathroom sinks). We would match the shades and mass-produce them and name them after their inventors. What a trip to have our advocates become co-creators.

The level of participation grew to mega proportions (out of our hands, actually). At one point I heard from Sephora and ULTA that there were these "strange women" showing up to our tester unit for hours each day to help out (strange, because they didn't work for us, and they didn't work for them either). Soon after, a big idea came across my desk: A group of customers was starting a Leslie's Angels program. In exchange for loads of product samples and the insider scoop, they'd continue to spread the word and give us seriously honest feedback. We agreed on one thousand members, and an original advocacy group was born.

It sounds a lot like what influencers of the 2020s do, except it didn't matter how many people they knew, it had nothing to do with their online profile, and they weren't being paid.

So why did they do it?

Because when you belong to something, you can have influence. Real community isn't about just following—it's about taking active ownership.

Get Yourself a Nine-Year-Old Mentor

58. To help us talk to customers in a new way about a new kind of foundation—one that let your skin shine through—we hired a new advisor: Téa Sloane.

Téa was nine years old—a whole year older than when she had asked me to be her mentor. She already had some experience running her duct-tape-wallet business when she was eight, so I took her on. Then a strange thing happened: As I taught her how running a company is like leading a band—you have to listen to each person like they are an instrument in a song—she taught me to pay closer attention to the language in makeup ads. Words like "flawless" and "perfect" to describe skin without "imperfections" suddenly jarred me into thinking, *What is an imperfection anyway, and how do you explain that to a young girl?* Téa had freckles (468 by her own count), and she loved all of them and didn't think any of them needed to be covered up.

So we hired Téa to advise our marketing and product-development teams. We had plenty of makeup experts, but what we didn't have was a freckle expert who could help us talk about letting your skin shine through when you have been told to cover it up your whole life.

Having been born with freckles, Téa told us they gave her personality and character and that they made her more adventurous and independent, like her role model, Jane Goodall, who also had freckles. "Just remember that," said Téa, "they are a part of you." It helped that she came prepared with handouts and a poster board. But what shined through her presentation was the power of her message: No one should tell you to cover yourself up. No one should tell you not to be confident. Nothing comes between your skin and your self-image. When you are nine.

To help inspire our customers to feel this way too, Téa helped us create a Facebook page called Freckles Rock—where we invited all those with freckles to celebrate the skin they were born in—a message we amplified internally by decorating our walls with their photos. All as an outgrowth of inviting a nine-year-old girl into our lives, a girl who did cartwheels through our halls when she wasn't sharing her honest views, inspiring all of us to express ourselves more freely and openly.

Which left me musing on the obvious: Why don't we do this more often? You don't need a new foundation—or *any* foundation—to bring a powerful new perspective into your life and work. You can learn a lot by listening to a kid.

Meet Téa Sloane and her 468 freckles.

Write Taglines for Fun

$59.$ Some people love crossword puzzles. Others like sudoku, French-braiding hair, or putting dogs in tutus. We all have things we like to do to simultaneously relax and sharpen our minds. I like creating names and taglines for new beauty products.*

Why do I do it? Because it helps me get past my creative blocks. It turns out to be a useful practice too.

Maybe you need to name something. A cat, a boat, a band, a brand. This is how I do it.

1. Sit down.
2. Think of what you need to name. (If you don't have anything and are doing this for the mental health benefits, consider using one of these ripe categories: candy bars, seafood restaurants, warm-up suits. Try anything you have a passion for.)
3. Find reading material.
4. Skim for good words.
5. Envision your word on a jar or package or promotion, and begin the tagline iteration.

Like these two (done on the fly):

* Thanks for indulging me here. My editor may or may not leave this item in.

145

Benevolence (as seen in a poem by Vijay Seshadri in *The New Yorker*)
Kind to your skin, tough on wrinkles

Upstage (as seen in the *New York Times*)
Outmaneuver premature wrinkles and get a front-row seat to fabulous skin.

Researchers have found that people who regularly do word puzzles show cognitive levels equal to that of someone *ten years younger.* They also have better grammar and better short-term memory. And you may surprise yourself with what you come up with. I've done a trademark search or two, just in case.

Oh, that's a good one:

Just in Case
The makeup case you leave in your car for those impulse buys at ULTA.

Some others from my files:

FacePlant
When your face meets the earth

Sci-fi Skincare
Why wait till 2045? Why not have your best skin now?
or
A lot of science and a little fiction

Einstein Skincare

You are smart enough to know that no magic cream is going to stop gravity from doing its thing to your face.

In the beauty product category, mascara names are the most fun. Here are some of mine:

Ridicu-lash

So ridiculously long, your glasses will protest

Daddy Long-Lash

Can you imagine a good-looking spider lady?

Long Live the Lashes

The king of mascara brands

Bushy lash

I could never get the team behind this one. A bunny with long lashes? No?

Your turn. Fill in the blank:

_____

Keep
Slathering

60. I collect creams. I get them in goody bags (a perk of being in my business). I buy them up at Bed Bath & Beyond. All sorts of creams, cheap ones and expensive ones. I use them to slather my hands, arms, neck (front and back), calves (yes, calves), thighs, lower back, elbows. Foot cream, hand cream, medicated cream—I don't care, and I don't necessarily put the cream where the jar specifies. I keep some on my nightstand. I keep some in my car and in my bag. Like a squirrel, I keep one buried in the yard.

Here's the deal: Everyone is always concerned about the neck up. People always forget about the neck down. But what's the neck attached to? Your body.

My rule is, if the cream is unproven and cheap, it always starts on body parts closest to the floor (i.e., feet, ankles, shins), and I work my way up. If it doesn't hydrate for many hours, the cream has failed me. If it works for days, even after a shower, it has won me over. Lavish by EVER skincare is one that moisturizes for the long haul. But no matter what, keep slathering. Why? If you keep slathering, your skin has lower odds of drying out and getting frail. You take control of your Skin's Dew Factor, or SDF (I made that up).

Not slimy, not sticky, not slick. Al dente.

Teeny Tiny Magic Moments*

61. I was running late to my meeting, panting up Sixth Avenue during the lunch-hour rush, weaving and bobbing around slowpokes like it was an Olympic sport,** when I crashed into a young woman carrying boxes stacked way above her head . . . that toppled onto mine.

I didn't say what I was thinking: *Why didn't YOU get out of MY way?* (Because I am a self-absorbed, impatient jerk who—*sometimes*—keeps her mouth shut.)

Which was a good thing: When the woman looked up, she smiled broadly and gave me a hug with her now-free arms. And she told me she loved our makeup and wore it every day.

* One alternate title for this book.
** See Nº69, Wired to Win.

Wow.

After we un-hugged and I helped her pick up her boxes, I walked the rest of the way to my meeting and savored the moment.

And here we are. Again.

I am a collector—of perfume,*** of photographs, of Teeny Tiny Magic Moments. My collection includes the time when our bareMinerals beauty bus was stopped by the police, and we dodged a ticket by inviting them inside for some fresh Krispy Kremes. And the time we ordered double espresso macchiatos at Starbucks in St. Louis from a gal named Kelly Reinhart, who gave us the best customer service of our lives, so we offered her a job on the spot to work at the bareMinerals boutique, and she took it. And the time I was just about to show a stranger who bumped into me on Sixth Avenue my worst side, and she showed me the best.

I do like to celebrate the big, Monumental Occasions, same as everybody else. But I don't like to wait for the big ones. Because magic is happening all the time, all around us. And if you make a point of looking out for Magic Moments— and remembering them—you will always have something to celebrate.

*** *See Nº66, Lead Yourself by the Nose.*

The
Two
Yous

62.

I was a person.

I was also a brand.

And we were confused.

The line between the brand and me had blurred, so if you hit a nerve in one, the other felt it. Like the time I found myself looking through the one-way glass at a focus group of women ripping the talent in our latest infomercial as "fake— *especially* her personality." And I ran into the room, screaming, "I'm the talent! I'm *real*!"

When you have a personal brand, how far do you want to go? No one can tell you where to stop. But you need a boundary. And only you can draw it.

- Know your brand.
- Know yourself.
- Know the difference.

There's a Tree Nearby

63.

After many years of running the company, I pulled back from daily operations, which gave me a lot more time to walk around my yard. It's a very short walk, only about five minutes, but somehow I had never found the time. And, therefore, I had never seen the tree: a huge, old, magnificent oak. In the middle of my yard. Twenty feet from my living room window.

How could I have missed this tree?! I LOVE trees. Trees are like people to me: They have roots, they're vertical, they have branches. But evidently, like people, trees are also easy to overlook—if you're me.

The tree just stood there, as though it had been standing there for one hundred years. (Which it had been.)

But I started shrinking. And the longer I looked at it, the smaller I felt.

And feeling small felt GOOD. To feel that the tree was here before me. That it will be here after me. It all works without me: the trees, the mountains, the moon, the *universe*. You're not the center of it, Leslie.

Take a moment to take that in. And revel in the freedom of being a tiny part of infinity. Find something really big that makes you feel really small—and full of wonder.

Find Your Jennifer

64. There are 1.7 million Jennifers living in the United States right now, which, if you like math, is about 33,000 Jennifers per state. Chances are, you know a Jennifer. Chances are, you *are* a Jennifer.

Let me tell you about mine. We met at the *Fortune* Most Powerful Women Conference, and Jennifer asked me to speak in her Power of Story class at Stanford. As a rule, I prefer risking death to public speaking,* but there was something otherworldly about her: She was intuitive, empathic, and blond. I gave her my card.

She changed my life.

* *See Nº81: Risk Taking for the Fearful.*

Here are a few things about Jennifer that enabled her to do this:

- She is a multiplier: Hope lives inside her, she spreads that hope to others, and she's intent on changing the world—and bringing others with her.
- She is fierce about reaching her goals without letting her ego get in the way.
- She can sprint in high heels, hike in flip-flops, and sit on the floor in a skirt.

The more I got to know her, the more I wondered—are ALL 1.7 million Jennifers like this? If so, shouldn't all of us tap into the Jennifer Ripple Effect?

Here is what I propose:

- If you know a Jennifer, hold her to her true potential, and get ready to grow.
- If you don't, find your Jennifer.
- And if you are a Jennifer, please, step up to the plate. It's like we've identified the MVP before the game: We already know you can do it! (And we're all counting on you.)

Block
It
Out

65.

I'm not actually sure this is good advice, but it has worked for me so far. Not necessarily as a principle or a value but as a method for moving on. If you're not ready to work through something, just forget it. Especially when the benefits of not remembering outweigh the hours of therapy to work it out.

For example:

- the time I cried while firing someone
- the speech(es) I bombed
- the evening I wore a stylish white leather pantsuit and was mistaken for a prostitute

And
Many
Many
More that I can't recall.

If the memory is not useful, it doesn't need to be remembered.

Lead Yourself by the Nose

66. According to one poll, more than half of all sixteen- to twenty-two-year-olds said they would rather give up their sense of smell than their smartphones and computers.

I am not a mental health professional. But as a person with both a nose and a smartphone, I think these people are making a mistake.

And they are not alone. Most of us don't fully appreciate our sense of smell. In fact, I'd bet many of us know more about our *sixth* sense than about using our fifth sense to its full power, or, really, its SUPER power, capable of taking us back in time—*and* of shaping our future.

Your nose is a spaceship that can travel through the space-time continuum, sending code to your brain that can sometimes trigger tears. Like the time I walked past a hyacinth bush in Santa Barbara and saw my grandmother (who had passed twenty years earlier) in a floral dress telling me to get my hair out of my face. You might think this was my sixth sense talking, but my ESP can't hold a scented candle to my scents memory.

Because your nose can take you back in time, it follows (if you understand how olfactory time travel works) that you can use scent *today* to create those memories (the *life*) that you will *want* to remember tomorrow.

You see, most scent-triggered trips in time are accidents. (Proust still would have remembered things past had his aunt given him my chocolate chip cookies instead of her madeleines.) Because most of us don't understand the mechanics of olfactory time travel. We know how to listen to music. We know how to watch movies. We know a massage feels good. And, boy, do we know how to eat. But how many of us know how to consciously USE scent?

Because I have collected scents my entire life, I know they have or *will* have significance.* My greatest memories can be brought back in a wrist dab, and using new scents gives me the opportunity to create new experiences that I can bring back in the future. So I use scent strategically, to set my intention:

- First, I don't have a signature scent. Would you eat the same food every day? Or listen to the same music? Baked ziti and ZZ Top for the rest of your life? Really?

---

* Recently I found a box in my basement with a fragrance I launched in a limited run more than twenty years ago, created by the trailblazing master perfumer Mandy Aftel. I am wearing it right now. It makes me deliriously happy.

- If I need a vacation, I will wear scent to bed to transport me somewhere. Often to an island.
- If I am facing a challenge, I might use a scent I wore in another challenging situation where I prevailed—as a kind of olfactory mnemonic support system.
- If I want an adventure, I might put on a new scent to encourage new behaviors. If you are going on a journey, why would you eat the same food you eat at home? (Yes, some people eat American hamburgers on vacation in Thailand. Just as some people would trade their nose for a smartphone. Please don't be those people.)

In conclusion, your nose is sticking out of your face for good reasons: to get there first, *then* to go back. Use your sense of smell to discover and create the life you want to remember. Lead yourself by the nose.

How to
Deliver
Shocking
News

67. My dear friend and entrepreneur Lisa Stone taught me something very important. When you have big news to deliver, you slap a "y'all" on the end to lessen the shock. I recommend saving this for special occasions. For example, Lisa is a member of the Bridge Group (see №95. Start a Bridge Group), so we're close, yet one day we all received this message over WhatsApp: "I'm married, y'all."

Now let's practice. Pick your favorite of the options below (or make up your own), and repeat it three times out loud, or until it sounds natural.

- I've peed my pants, y'all.
- I'm becoming a monk, y'all.
- I'm going to jail, y'all.

Congratulations, again, to Lisa and Christopher!

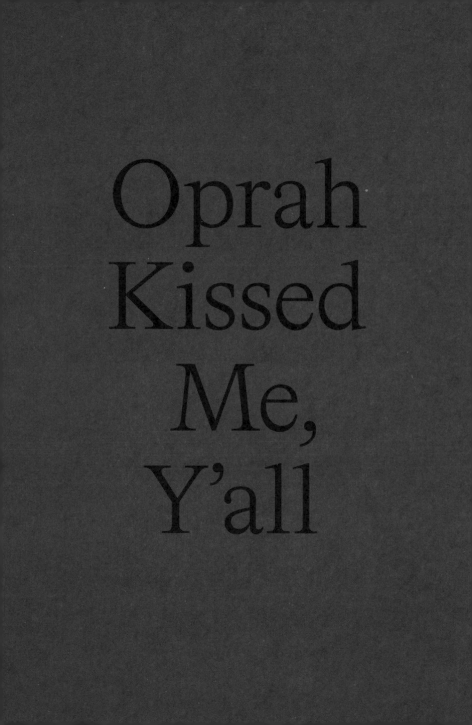

Oprah Kissed Me, Y'all

68.

I have shocking news. I met Oprah. And she kissed me.

Why would Oprah do that? Because I asked her to.

Why would I ask her to? Because—and excuse me in advance for sounding totally nuts—three years after meeting Oprah I think I am ready to demystify what I received from her that day: When her hand held mine, I felt her energy enter my bloodstream, and I felt a sense of calm (because I wasn't calm). I felt connected. I felt *inspired.**

I believe what happens with Oprah is that she attaches herself to this massive power source, then infuses that energy into other people through her words, her actions, and this time just her touch. I felt the force loud and clear.

And I followed her example; I used her personal power as a catalyst to tap my own. And to go for it. By asking for a kiss. And then a favor: As I was saying goodbye, I told her about a super fan who was celebrating her fiftieth birthday. Oprah got excited and told me to pull out my phone to video her birthday message.

Like doing a whole 21-Day Meditation Experience with Oprah and Deepak. (This is not an ad.)

Here is what she said:

Hello, it's me. Oprah. I hear you're turning fifty. Let me just tell you something. It is the best—did you hear me?—THE BEST time of your life. Because the fifties are everything that you've thought of and that you've been meaning to be. It's a time where everything RISES to the moment, and you don't give two pouts about what other people have to say about who you are. It means that you rise into the fullness of yourSELF. You get to step up and step out into your life in a way that you never have before. So happy birthday. Happy birthday. Happy NEW LIFE is what it really is. And don't let anybody give you any crap about what it means to turn fifty, 'cause it is THE GREATEST. I'm telling you.

If you haven't turned fifty, don't worry: You don't have to wait! Personal power is a choice at any age. You are never too young—and never too old—to rise up to the opportunity of the moment.

Wired
to Win

69. I was invited to Necker Island in the British Virgin Islands to meet with a group of super-sharp, bootstrapping entrepreneurs. This island had lemurs and pink flamingos and a gift shop where I bought every one of Richard Branson's memoirs. We swapped business stories, discussed how to save the coral reefs, and had fun too. Like the costume party where we dressed like something you would find at the bottom of the sea (I wore seaweed-green eye shadow on my lips).

One clear night, we split up into small groups for a midnight catamaran race under the stars. These were type-A personalities who took performance seriously. A race to this group meant only one thing: victory.

I was fumbling with my life jacket while my team dashed to the boat; our rivals were already flying along the rippled surface, leaving us in their wake. It was mayhem.

We found ourselves trying every angle to catch the wind while our competition was already at the bar drinking margaritas. We were alone out there. We stopped hustling. We looked up. There were a million stars piercing the sky, and one bright moon reflecting light off the dark sea and onto our faces, where the weight of defeat started to transform into something else. A stillness. The boat rocked gently with the waves, and everyone grew quiet. The only sound was the flapping of the sail against the mast. And then it hit us.

Not the mast. An idea: Maybe we were looking at winning all wrong.

Competition is one of the most powerful drivers, but sometimes you may need to chart a different course.

Sail your own race.

Make Discovery Routine

70.

When you stop trying new things is when you start getting old and bitter and basically dead.

Saying no to the new becomes a lifestyle. That little happiness you used to feel about trying new stuff? Now it's anger—anger at yourself because you don't know how to do it anymore, anger at others because they do.

So don't let your comfort zone become your dead zone. I'm not saying go skydiving or bungee jumping (I would never go bungee jumping). Just make discovery routine.

My Comfort Zone

71. I have this place. A room, actually, on the small side, with a cozy hot pink velvet sofa, which is soft but not too soft. One wall displays my favorite books and the books I have never read but always wanted to. The adjacent wall is covered in color, every color you can think of and ones you have never seen before because they are too rare for most human eyes. It has a sound system that would blow your mind. The gentle vibrational rhythms float into the atmosphere and morph with the melted-chocolate aroma rising from the

homemade cookies baking in the oven. Together, they create an olfactory sound (you heard that right) that a unicorn makes when it is in ecstasy. On a side table is a plate of fast-food French fries, always crisp, always piping hot, always within arm's reach.

When I am in that room, I can't bear to leave. But if I don't, I never would. This place, of course, lives inside my imagination and is called MCZ, My Comfort Zone.

The comfort zone is a seduction, but it's not real. It's a fantasy made up by that little spot in your brain that wants you to miss the not-to-be-missed experiences of your life. Sometimes I daydream about MCZ, and I want it so badly that I can practically smell the cookies.

Sometimes I have the willpower to check in for a time and then scram before I get sucked in. But I always find that the times I am able to avoid it completely are when I give myself some slack and tell myself that the knot in the pit in my stomach that comes when I am uncomfortable is temporary and always goes away.

So do what I do. Acknowledge your comfort zone and use it when it feels right—when you need to breathe—but don't stay too long, 'cause it may be a fine place to visit, but you wouldn't want to live there.

Unwinding (a.k.a. Find Your Own Meditation)

72. I like to be first on the buffet line. I press the elevator button multiple times. And, yes, that's me riding your bumper. Keith would say I am a little wound up. But I do know how to unwind. All I need is a crochet needle and a ball of yarn.

My mother taught me how to crochet in elementary school, and since then crocheting has come to the rescue many times. Like last winter, when I moved into an apartment near Stanford to become a DCI (Distinguished Careers Institute—imagine!) Fellow, a yearlong program for people to renew their sense of purpose. This was alien terrain: I could not find the syllabus or my classroom or a barista. So after each disorienting day on campus spent dodging eighteen-year-old cyclists away from home for the first time, each night I would go back to my pad, curl up on my extra-firm rental sofa, and settle into my groove with a no. 5 hook and colorful wool: following YouTube videos and online patterns, yarning over, pulling through loop after loop . . . slowing myself down through the calming, hypnotic repetition of making granny squares.

These days I don't wait for a panic attack to start me making a blanket or a bunny. It is part of my routine meditation on patience. It's also fun! Best of all, if you start crocheting now, you can make your dog a scarf for his birthday.

Me crocheting an
afghan in 1983

Adaptation
Is
Power

73.

There is transformative power in adapting to what irks you about yourself. An oyster may wish that grain of sand would go away.* But any oyster worth its salt water gets to work adapting. Which is worth remembering every time you see a string of pearls.

* Who really knows what oysters wish?

Don't Let the Sunshine In

74. In case you haven't heard, the sun can do bad things to your skin. That's why most beauty professionals avoid tanning like the plague: We know the number-one way to look older is to bake ourselves.

I didn't know this growing up. When I was a kid on Long Island, we would spend summers working on our tans, then line up our arms from elbows to wrists to compare progress. Yes, I had the Mediterranean genetic advantage over my fair-skinned Germanic friends—but I also worked harder: This was back in the 1970s, when there was no sunscreen, just suntan oil with SPF 2. So starting in May, I smelled like coconuts. By the time August rolled around, I looked like a slice of pumpernickel. It was awe-inspiring—if sizzling your largest organ floats your boat.

Then one day in my mid-twenties, while I was sunbathing in Florida, the pumpernickel turned beet red. My skin was telling me to stop. I listened.

Today, I never leave home without sunscreen, even on my hands. I wear long sleeves during the day in summer, especially on the beach. And I own a ton of hats. I do look foolish sometimes.* But bedspread-head beats turning red—or dead.** And if I need a little extra color, the fake stuff comes off in the shower.

Me at my niece Sydney's college graduation with my son, Trent. There were no seats left under the tent.

**Ultraviolet radiation from the sun is the number-one cause of skin cancer.*

Three Easy Ways to Look Older Than You Are

75.

1. Don't wear sunscreen.
2. Never laugh at yourself.
3. Be bitter.

Your
Heroes
Are
Insecure

76.

Ever wish you were more like your role models? Be careful what you wish for! Over the years I have spent time with many of mine—at conferences, at social events, in all sorts of places. So I can tell you from personal experience, your role models have as many insecurities as the rest of us. Just because you can't see someone's weaknesses doesn't mean they don't have any. It means they're human: flawed but good at concealing!*

* *Makeup comes in many forms.*

Chasing
Goose
Bumps

77. I didn't talk much when I left the theater after seeing *Hamilton*, the musical. All I know is, I was a changed woman. "What the heck just happened?" was all I could muster.

In a matter of hours, I had watched Lin-Manuel Miranda unhinge an institution and change the way stories were told. It's not just that he didn't follow the rules—it was more like he didn't know there were rules to follow.

It blindsided me. Pre-*Hamilton*, I didn't even realize my creativity was waning. Post-*Hamilton*, I woke up. I discovered that I missed being rapt, fascinated, intrigued. The musical knocked me out of my creative doldrums. It reminded me that feeling awe is at the core of originality. I get goose bumps just thinking about it.

Hamilton moved me to action. All of a sudden I was writing raps and performing them in public, ordering the U.S. Constitution from Amazon and visiting Mount Vernon. The show was like a master class in how someone's passion can ignite imagination in others.

Don't risk becoming a dud. Get out of your head, away from your computer, and let the unexpected change you.

When You're in Line for Coffee

78. When you're in line for coffee (or tea), what do you normally do? Check your phone? Complain about the line? Consider buying a mug?

Next time you're in line at the coffee shop, try something new: Give somebody a compliment. Look around you, notice something unique-looking about somebody, and tell them about it. Do it daily. They feel great, you feel great, and it sets the tone for the rest of your day (or at least the rest of your wait in that line).

Bear in mind that compliments don't work if you only think them. If you see something, say something. I've been seated at a restaurant and walked all the way across the room to tell someone that I loved their dress. I realize I risked looking like a nut, but why hold back? Another thing: Don't be a phony. You have to really mean it, because fakers are *the worst*.

How to Receive a Compliment

79. OK, now I'm going to suggest you learn how to receive compliments. Try it out the next time someone compliments you while you're waiting in line for coffee.

Let's start by remembering the last time you received a compliment. Close your eyes and think of what it was. *Love your purple hair, nice snakeskin belt, what a handsome pet frog you have.*

Remember how good you felt? Remember how long that feeling lasted? If it didn't last more than half a day, I'm going to suggest you book an appointment with your life coach.

Now, let's remember what you said in response. Were you effusive? Or did you say, "Oh, thanks," or "This old thing?" and deflect or deny? No good. The next time you get a compliment, here's what I want you to do: You say, "Oh, my gosh, thank you so much! Wow, you made my day." Then you get the attention of whomever you're with (or text a family member, even if you know it will interrupt them in a meeting) and you say, "Did you hear that? This person just said (insert compliment)!" If this level of enthusiasm is not for you, you can also be specific and direct. Like this:

> *Stranger: "I love your scarf."*
> *Leslie: "Thanks so much. It was $7.99 at*
> *T.J. Maxx."*

This is how you make it the most memorable compliment that person has ever given, which makes them want to do it again for somebody else.* And that, my friend, is how you change the world.

---

* Please note, this practice may result in hugging strangers. This is good for you.

Humor Time Travel

Humor is tragedy plus time.*
—Mark Twain

80. Reframing stories with humor is a great way to transform unsavory episodes into comic gold—even if it is only for your sanity. I had an urgent opportunity to put this idea into practice two days before Christmas last year. I was with my family at the annual Charles Dickens reenactment festival, when I saw the Ghost of Christmas Past:

* I have been a big fan of Mark Twain for years, but I found this quote after I had already come to the same conclusion, I swear.

my family . . . not getting along . . . just like the last Christmas . . . and the Christmas before that.

We all know that family and holidays have the potential to be disastrous, and I was not willing to play Scrooge this year. While the haunting scene was unfolding before me, I decided to picture myself one year from then, when I would be howling with laughter at the retelling of the tale. It was hard. I had to reason with my impulses. *Stay with it. This is comedy*, I told myself as I popped a vein in my neck.

The details aren't important (I don't want to talk about it**). The point is that this could have ruined me for the rest of the month, but it didn't. Why wait to find the humor in an ugsome*** situation? Don't lash out; instead, lie back and enjoy, 'cause this shit is funny.

** *See Nº65. Block It Out.*

*** *Charles Dickens liked this word. He borrowed it from Old Norse (for further reading on etymology, see Nº82. For the Love of Words).*

Risk Taking for the Fearful

81. According to my research, three out of four people suffer from "glossophobia,"* the legit word for fear of public speaking. I have no idea if this is actually true, but if it is, you probably are one of those three. Welcome to the club.

If you're trying to shake this fear, let me tell you what doesn't work. Early in my TV shopping days, I tried to overcome my fear of public

Am I the only one who thought this meant fear of lip gloss?

speaking using my fear of heights. My theory being, if I could jump past my acrophobia and parachute out of an airplane, my glossophobia would see I was willing to kill us all if it didn't release me from its snare.

Then my parachute didn't open. My little dot of a young son looking up at me from the ground started getting really big, really fast as I dropped like a rock from the sky. And by the time my backup parachute opened and I landed, my glossophobia—AND my acrophobia—knew they'd won: I thanked God, out loud, for being safe and sound in the arms of my child.

In other words, my experiment failed: I still dread public speaking. (And I am still afraid of heights.) And I'm OK with that. Because if there's one thing I'm REALLY afraid of—and I think this fear is healthy—it's not growing. And sometimes making progress means making peace with things you cannot change.

Me skydiving
(after the backup
chute opened)

For the Love of Words

82. You may not know this from reading my book, but I love words. My problem is, I don't know so many. To be fair, I do have a million words in my fantasy life.* I just have trouble finding them in real life.

So a few years ago, I got an online subscription to the Oxford English Dictionary. I took a course called The Secret Life of Words. I started following @MerriamWebster on Twitter. And I signed up to get Word of the Day in my inbox; e.g., "muse, to think." Which—I never would have thought—led me to the "etymology" (another word I didn't know) for "Muses," whose shrine was a "Museum," which I didn't know either—even though I like thinking and going to museums. I also like eating "apples," which as late as the seventeenth century was

* The average vocabulary for an English-speaker is twenty thousand words—one reason this is a fantasy.

a generic term for *all* fruit, except berries but including nuts. Which really *is* nuts. And so on.

I love words. They're like a steamy love affair with benefits. That's why my rock stars are novelists, poets, biographers, and lyricists—because, my God, they know their way around a dictionary. How do they find the exact right word and put it in a sentence and make people cry? Or laugh? Or *muse*?

Think about it: Singers can't sing without lyrics. History can't exist without stories. And then there is *Moby-Dick* by Herman Melville, the novel about Captain Ahab's quest for revenge on a white whale, which everyone at Stanford says is *the* great American novel and someone online called a great American love story.

I can't say, because I haven't read it. It's on my nightstand, and there are LOTS of words in it, which I find *daunting*. But I do know what happens at the end, and if that's a love story, it would be pretty *ironic*: Your lover rips off your leg, then drowns you at the bottom of the ocean? Another reason to be grateful for Keith!

In the meantime, I'm following @MobyDickatSea, which tweets out lines from the novel to lure you in. For example, "Such things may seem incredible; but, however wondrous, they are true."

Which brings to mind another favorite word: *awe.*

George Washington & Me

83. There's nothing like a good biography to teach you about history and character. Like Ron Chernow's *Washington: A Life*, which tells you EVERYTHING you ever wanted to know about our first president.

Obviously, George was a pretty accomplished guy. But what I love most about him are his flaws—those nagging issues that could have held him back but didn't stop him from carrying on with the big stuff, like winning the war against the British.

Seeing quirks in those we admire is affirming. It reminds us that the challenges we face are surmountable.

So, what is it about GW that gives me hope?

1. He had a love-hate relationship with his mother, whom he could never please, no matter how many battles he won.
2. He had unusually large hips for his build and needed special trousers made for him in London.
3. He knew image was everything and kept his appearance meticulous with that cute little black ribbon in his ponytail, even during the frigid days when his soldiers were dying of frostbite.

So, I feel better about myself because I have some things in common with George Washington. If he could deal with Benedict Arnold, then I could certainly deal with my HR issues.

A bust of GW I keep in my home office

For Further Reading: *Rules of Civility*

84.

GW didn't leave home without the right outfit or the right accessory. Namely, *110 Rules of Civility & Decent Behavior in Company and Conversation*. The founding father of advice books.

Here are my favorites:

- *Roll not the eyes.*
- *Bedew no man's face with your spittle by approaching too near him when you speak.*
- *When in company, put not your hands to any part of the body not usually discovered.*
- *If you soak your bread in the sauce, let it be no more than what you put in your mouth at a time.*
- *Give not advice without being asked & when desired do it briefly.*

I can't include much more, but you can buy it from Amazon for $3.76.

It's a
Sign

85. One day, we woke up and couldn't open our front door.* The lock had jammed, and no locksmith in the area could repair it. Even Keith, who can fix anything, was stumped.

I took this as a sign. And I don't mean a sign telling me DON'T do something, like a black cat crossing my path. I mean a sign TO DO something: Stop isolating ourselves socially and invite people inside. So we had a huge party, and when guests arrived, *they* saw a sign: DETOUR. PLEASE ENTER THRU SIDE DOOR.

Signs are everywhere, and it's your job to figure out what they're trying to say. Maybe the mattress on the side of the road is telling you to get more sleep. Or go to the chiropractor. Or to buy a new mattress.

Whatever the sign, open up to the opportunity, and steer clear of superstition. If I see a black cat cross the road in front of me, for example, I keep driving and call the salon—it's a sign I need to get my roots done.

* *If we didn't have other doors to our house, we might still be locked in.*

You're Alive.
Yay.
Now Go
Read
Obituaries

86. It all started in my bedroom as a kid. I would turn out the lights and read the obituaries in Long Island's *Newsday* on the floor of my room by the flicker of my strawberry-scented votive candles.

You might think this sounds morbid, but reading obituaries makes you think about what people will remember about you. You wonder: *Who were these people? What was their story? What are people going to say about ME when I'm gone? Oh, wow. Maybe that's something I could actually work on NOW?*

How do you want people to remember you?

I might want a billboard.* But I don't want a government holiday or a tombstone—or even an urn. Just ashes that the people who loved me can spread somewhere in nature to remember how I lived.**

I've taken a lot of marching orders on living from the dead, by reading obituaries and biographies. To the point that when someone reads my obituary one day, they—hopefully!—will think, *That's a pretty good way to live.* It's possible they will learn how *not* to live. But—knock on wood—I still have a few more years to read more obituaries and biographies and get ideas for how to live a more meaningful life.

* *Or a footnote.*

** *Just don't spread them in water—no oceans or lakes or rivers or built-in pools. And not near the mall. Ideally an earthy patch in Northern California, preferably in the mountains but not too high.*

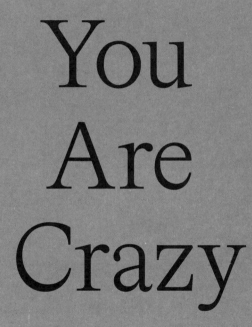

87.

Last week I was shopping at Bergdorf's, and I found these rhinestone hair clips that spelled out words: WOMAN. BOSS. CRAZY. I couldn't find ME. But I shelled out two hundred bucks anyway (which really *was* crazy!), because it's a sign* that the world is catching up to what you and I have known for a long time: When you are everyone else's go-to problem solver/ultimate optimist/rock while you are also trying to keep your own life together, your battery never stops, even if you do. Which can be exhausting to the point of losing it.

So the next time you feel nuts, remember: You're complex, you take chances, and you don't let little things hold you back. And in this world, that kind of courage and confidence IS crazy!**

* *See N°85. It's a Sign.*

** *My friend the esteemed entrepreneur Linda Rottenberg (also known as La Chica Loca) wrote a whole book about this called* Crazy Is a Compliment.

Holding
Butterflies

88. When I moved to the Bay Area, I thought I should give trail running a shot. The more rocks and places to twist my ankle, the better.

Eventually my back started bothering me, and I had to take time off. Then I went to a ChiRunning coach, who told me running can be pain-free if you have good form, which mostly means being relaxed.

"Relaxed?!"

"Visualize holding butterflies," he told me. Versus imagining you're a pouncing California puma dressed in bright pink running tights.

So I reimagined my puma pounce as a calm stag's leap. And the next time I tripped on the trail (I think I was too relaxed), I rolled back up to my feet.

So, hold butterflies—then let 'em go.

Collect
to
Connect

---

89. There was a time in my not-too-distant past when I housed about 800 bareMinerals eye shadows in my home. Please don't worry about me, because I am now down to 287. So I know a bit about collecting (which can also look just like not throwing stuff away). Keith pays rent on two* storage units to hold the stuff I can't part with.

* OK, three.

I am not alone in my passion—and *that's* the point. Collecting bareMinerals eye shadows was an obsession I shared with customers and employees alike—thousands of women across the country—all of us showing pictures of our little pots to one another online. Which brought us closer together: We would name shades after these women, they'd name shades for us, sometimes they would develop their own blends that we would launch and give them creative credit for, and around and around we'd go—connecting through our shared love of makeup.

And connection, in the end, is what I value most—and I need physical reminders of it. Not so many that when I die the fire department needs to come in because no one can find me. Just enough to remember how I felt. I collect to connect to moments of joy.

I think Marie Kondo and I should be friends, to be honest. From what I hear, we're opposites in some ways, and we could be good for each other. She could help me downsize. And I could give her a photo of the two of us in my newly emptied storage unit . . . to remind her of the joy when we connected.

Glisten Up

90.

It really ticks me off when beauty experts tell women over forty that shimmery eye makeup will make them look old.

My rule is: There are no rules. Especially when it comes to how you want to present yourself to the world. No one should tell you what to do with your own body. I am (way) over forty. I own 287 glimmer eye shadows.

This goes way beyond shimmer. When you start questioning the rule-makers and learn to make judgments from personal experience and practice, you empower yourself. Question beauty authority figures (including me). Question authority figures. Makeup your own mind.

P.S. When I see women with glimmer, I can tell they are full of joie de vivre. These people are also often awesome dancers and have great taste in shoes. And they're the type to spot crappy advice from a mile away.

Pretty, shimmery pots

Be Like Sophia Loren

91. Sometimes it really helps to see a beauty icon in the flesh. A couple of years ago, my husband and I went to Sophia Loren's eightieth-birthday party in Napa. We mingled among the other esteemed guests (we were invited because we knew the caterer), and I particularly enjoyed the live music and spotting gorgeous outfits. While we sipped the finest local Chardonnay and nibbled on foraged mushrooms, I noticed Robert Redford's strawberry blond hair from a distance, but it was Sophia I was dying to see up close.

Lucky for me, Sophia and I were on the same schedule, and I was right behind her in line for the porta potty. She was still a bombshell. Remember those old movies with the quintessential look of Vaseline on the camera lens? Sophia Loren had that fuzzy quality about her in person. She was blurry in a lovely way. I was taken by her ability to retain sex symbol status at her age. Before her handler could stop me, I pulled out my iPhone and snapped a few pics of her feet. I also got her head. But her feet intrigued me. *How does she wear heels at her age?*

I committed everything about her look to memory, because I knew I could take cues that I could apply to myself when I'm her age. I'm a planner. And, a few years ago, I decided that I would be proactive in shaping my identity as an older person. These are secrets I have shared with no one—until now.

Here's what I learned from Sophia. Tips for what to wear to a big event when you're eighty—or you have errands to run:

- Large tinted indoor/outdoor glasses, with fade lenses so you can still see the eyes.
- Heels about two inches high. Sensible and chunky. No spikes.
- Black elegant ankle-length gown, but not too long or you'll trip.
- Sheer fabric over décolleté and arms. (Bonus points for little sparkly crystals to play with the light.)

Makeup Assignment

92.

LEARN TO LOVE YOURSELF
IN MAKEUP.

LEARN TO LOVE YOURSELF
WITHOUT MAKEUP.

That is all.

Beautiful Contradictions

Do I contradict myself?
Very well then I contradict myself;
(I am large, I contain multitudes.)
—Walt Whitman,
"Song of Myself," *Leaves of Grass*

93.

At a certain point, I gave up on trying *not* to contradict myself. I found there's beauty in contradiction. You are allowed to change your mind. Or have radically different answers for different situations. That's not crazy. That's human.

For example, all the following contain truth:

Get in the habit of saying yes.	Get comfortable saying no.
Routine is grounding.	Routine kills.
Stand out.	Blend in.
Speak up.	Stop talking.
Live in the moment.	Set goals.
Loosen up.	Be diligent.
Don't be so emotional.	Feel stuff.
Trust your intuition.	Be suspicious of those "gut feelings."

It is equally true that when you change your mind, some people will brand you as "Inconsistent!"

To which I say, "Thank you!"

Sometimes.

Fifty-Four Bunnies

94. One morning when I was on a run in the Marin Headlands with stunner views of the Pacific Ocean, I saw a bunny hopping beside me on the hilly trail. She was fluffy and floppy and had a camo thing going for her as she blended in with the dried grass, then hopped away.

I carried on my run and saw a second bunny twitching his little brown nose, which inspired me to pick up the pace. And I saw a third bunny. And a fourth.

Then I did what any Homo sapiens does when privileged to be the solitary witness to you've-got-to-see-it-to-believe-it, can't-wait-to-tell-others-you-saw-it insanely overwhelming cuteness: I started counting bunnies. Nine, twelve, eighteen, twenty-six, thirty-four. It was wondrous. Supernatural. Bunny heaven!

Just when I thought I had counted the last bunny, another would hop onto the trail. Then hop off. On. Off. And I was flying.

By the time I got back home, I was in a state of euphoria, like I'd spoken to God, as I told Keith about my miraculous morning. "I counted fifty-four bunnies!"

"Are you sure it wasn't the same bunny?" asked my mere-mortal husband.

"Not the same bunny! Different bunnies! Fifty-four *different* bunnies!"

Bunnies that must have hopped around the Headlands for days, I realized after cooling down from my post-run run-in—long before I finally saw them.

Which set me wondering: What else am I missing? What other miracles are hiding in plain sight?

One insanely cute bunny should probably be proof enough. But sometimes it takes fifty-four bunnies to remind you to look more closely and you will see that everything is a miracle. Even, and especially, a lovable skeptic who actually believes that one bunny with three-inch legs could keep up with ME for six miles in the Marin Headlands. Now THAT would be a miracle!

Start a Bridge Group

94.

Make time for relationships.
—Lisa Edwards*

When I turned fifty, Keith and Trent took me to Napa for a delicious lunch and an outdoor art exhibit complete with roaming peacocks. It was a wonderful day with my two favorite men. Who talked about cars—not the book I was reading or that day's update from my new astrology app.

Not that I needed to talk to them about any of that. But these were things I cared about. And I wondered if it was possible to have friendships with people who cared about these things too—women people who might appreciate my interests and talents, like eating popcorn with chopsticks.

Up until then, I hadn't prioritized friendship. I had been surrounded by female energy every day in the office for years, and I was still close with the girlfriend-customer community that had developed when we scaled the company. All of those business trips and the pressures of running a company while raising a kid had been enough.

* *Pretty good advice from one of our Bridge Group members. (More of these gems to come.)*

Now that kid was twenty-one—my personal life centered on two grown men. Who were watching me blow out candles on a lovely birthday cake, three of us sitting at a table for four.

∞

> Take bigger risks.
> —Jennifer Aaker

When my friend Jennifer invited me to a stranger's home for a sleepover in Bodega Bay with nine other women, seven of whom I had never met, I had reservations:

1. Overnight is a long time.
2. Would I be sharing a room?
3. Did I own cute pj's?

But I had been diving into novel experiences for two years at this point, so I said yes. And I drove across the bridge.

There was no talk of creating a group that weekend. We were just ten women who had left the dogs, kids, and men at home so we could walk on the beach and talk frankly.

Then out came the wine. Someone hung a portable disco ball. And I found myself dancing like I was fifteen—with women who had families and careers and LIVES.

Jennifer had been musing for a while about creating a group of girlfriends like her mom's bridge group—which had been meeting for fifty years for cards and conversation—only without cards. But we all lived in the Bay Area—you have to take bridges to go anywhere. And *to bridge* is *to connect*. So the name still worked.

∞

It's the quality of engagement,
not the number of hours.
—Joanna Drake

Like most women, everyone in the Bridge Group is BUSY. To make the most of our time together, we have rules:**

- Meet four times a year, starting in January.
- Before your first meeting, fill out a Google doc with your personal goals and a six-word story that sums up your intentions, and share these in person.
- At subsequent meetings, compare your personal goals with your progress, which will inspire you and help others hold you accountable.

** *Yes, we run the Bridge Group basically like a start-up. Because CEOs on the beach are still CEOs, only with sand between their toes.*

- Note how your personal goals support and are supported by the group's mission: *We are a defined tribe of badass, wise girlfriends who have a social contract to strengthen, lift, nurture, celebrate, and dare one another on life's journey.*
- We operate with an abundance mind-set.***
- Between in-person meetings, share news—ups, downs, *stuff*—on a daily basis, by text. Even if all you do is read the thread, you will feel connected.

∞

We are never alone.
—Jamie Gardner

Our primary rule is to show up: no judgment, no drama, no slackers. This is a *commitment.* You can't flake.

In return, you get real friends with real benefits:

- Practical—when you face any challenge, your group contains many more potential solutions than you can think up on your own.
- Physical—people with friends live longer.

*** *Except for free time, which is as scarce as water in the Sahara.*

- Emotional/psychological—when you know that nine badass women have your back no matter what, guess how that makes you feel?

We talk about everything, to help one another through anything: With ten people in the group, we are never all going through a crisis at the same time, so the group always has enough positive energy to help its members heal.

Building a bridge that can help you rise up and over any challenge takes work. So we put the same rigor into the Bridge Group as we put into our careers. But we also took our time. To go big, start small.

∞

Be kind to everyone, starting with yourself.
—me*

My Bridge Group

Marriage
Is a
Multiplex

96. My marriage is like a multiplex. A theater with many screens, playing a romance, a drama, a period piece, and something directed by Jordan Peele, where you're not sure whether to laugh or cry. Of course, when we were starting out, it was rom-com bliss all day every day.

Keith and I have changed over the years. People grow; people grow up. When we met, I was just beginning my career. We didn't know where I was headed, and we certainly didn't envision Keith putting his career aspirations aside to be the lead parent.* But he was willing to go for it, and that's part of the beauty of this partnership—even though he was raised in a traditional household, he didn't have hang-ups around gender roles.

We had our agreements, and we disagreed too, but that was normal. We've been married over thirty years, and I tell KB that we will be that adorable old couple holding hands on the street thirty years from now. (Probably trying to find our apartment.)

Here is what I know so far:

- Marriage requires patience. Listening more, interrupting less. I had heard this years ago, but I am just getting good at it.

* *Thanks for this new term, Sally Thornton.*

- Marry someone who makes you laugh, and keep it up. Shelving your sense of humor is a lot easier than keeping it fresh. Keith and I watch comedy at night, not the news, not a slasher flick. We always agree on that.
- You don't need to be alike. We embrace our differences. I freak out. He remains calm. He keeps volatility at bay. I keep colorful wigs in the closet. He watches Formula 1. I leave the room. We cover more ground this way.

We were inseparable early on, but over the years having personal time and space became essential to the health of our relationship, because we all need to be alone sometimes to work things out. The kitchen became KB's sanctuary. Eating home-cooked meals is when we come together to talk, or not, depending on what we both need.

And we travel, experiencing newness together and collecting shared memories (we take turns remembering details).

It's pretty simple. We respect each other. Our choices, our decisions, our dreams. It's also complicated,** like a good psychological thriller; usually KB has it figured out in the first thirty minutes, and I need to watch till the end.

On our wedding day, in a conference room in the Time & Life Building, in New York City

** See Nº93: Beautiful Contradictions.

At the End of the Day

97. When Tish's husband, Mauro, called and asked, "Could you speak to my wife?" I had no idea what to say. *How did I get here? Is this what naturally happens when the line blurs between your work life and your personal life? When your work IS your life?*

"OK," I said. And Mauro held the phone to Tish's ear.

Starting at Macy's, I've always tried to put myself in the shoes of the women who would stop by the makeup counter. Hearing their stories and finding common ground with them allowed me to serve women in ways that never felt like work. Years later, the company we built was really about *keeping company* with these women. Our shared love of little pots of makeup was just a starting point for sharing our passions, which led to relationships that got deeper, stronger, more personal.

When you're driven by love, when do you stop? Love, by definition, is unreasonable. It drives you to bring a relentless intensity to what you do. Not because you are told to or even because you *want* to. Because you have to. It can make you a little intense. But the beauty is, it also drives you to go beyond your limitations, beyond your fears and failures. It's an invitation to go beyond *yourself,* to places you may not understand at first but that ultimately feel right.

So when I got the call from Mauro asking me to speak to Tish in her final hours, even if I didn't feel exactly "qualified," it felt like a natural progression of the journey we'd been on together for a long time. I knew how much our community meant to Tish, because it meant that much to *me*. It was a place where you could talk about *anything*: your best moments, your worst moments, even—I was reluctantly discovering—your last moments.

My heart was pounding. What do you say to a thirty-nine-year-old beauty who is in a coma and isn't going to make it?

You thank her. For what she has given you. For her positive attitude and her humor and her style that always put us all at ease. For the little things she did to make your life better—even as she herself battled for her life. For how she inspired you, and everyone who knew her, to become better.

There are many measures of success in this world. And as the former CEO of a public company, I've been judged by a lot of them: revenue, gross margin, quarterly earnings, and so on. The pressure to measure up is relentless and unforgiving. But that's not what I remember from my corner office. It's the people I got to know. And how they changed me.

Many years ago, when I started down this road, I wasn't sure where it was going to lead. Now I know.

When Mauro spoke of Tish's life in his eulogy, he was also telling the story of my life: of a woman who loved makeup not just because it made her feel beautiful, but because the friendships she formed around it made her feel invincible. Of course, one price of admission to such joy can be the aching vulnerability that comes from facing one another's frailties. But for me, being asked to say goodbye to Tish is one of the proudest moments of my life. It was a moment that was twenty years in the making, yet still I felt utterly unprepared, which confirms one of my fundamental beliefs as a human being: No fear is powerful enough to stop you if you are driven by love.

Love
Rules

I have this necklace that spells out L-O-V-E. It's six inches wide across my chest, and you can spot it from across the room. I wear it often, especially in settings where I don't know a soul. I started noticing that when people see my necklace, their eyes light up, their shoulders ease up, and the corners of their mouth turn up. My LOVE necklace is so audacious that it breaks the ice. Because it's kind of funny and kind of true. I imagine it is because love is always on our minds, but we don't always know when it is in our midst. I think we can all agree that when it shows up, we are just plain relieved.

Love is pretty much my story. I do not believe the company I helped build would have made such an impact if all the people who touched the brand didn't know how to love, and not just other people but experiences, concepts, and ideas. We didn't believe love needed to be reserved for special occasions or special people. You can love the color blue and not dilute the nature of love. Love, when used liberally, hits home. It's true I brought my emotions to work, and sometimes my passion was over the top, too much, sometimes so real it was raw. I don't regret having those feelings. Emotions drive connection.

We all have the capacity to love. We need it to survive, and one thing I know for sure is that we all just want to be loved.

Use your heart. Believe in love.

Thank you from the bottom of my heart.

Love,
Leslie
XOX

Acknowledgments

To be honest, I have never read the acknowledgments section of anyone's book, but now that I know why it exists I plan to go back and read them all. It's the part where the author shows their gratitude and thanks those people closest to them, although I'm still a little confused about whether I am supposed to thank people who helped make this book a reality like the incredible Campbell "Millennial" Schnebly, the top dog who literally got this book onto the pages, and colorful Carlye Adler, who was there every day with Campbell. And the wonderful Lindsay Edgecombe, my agent, and spirited Holly Dolce, my editor. And of course there is James Braly, who has been writing with me for six years, and Bassima Mroue, who pulled out sticky notes with chapter titles many years ago, and John Evans, who was my writing teacher at Stanford, and Joe Dworetzky, who told me the truth. Or am I supposed to thank people in my life who helped me get here to this amazing place and space I am in right now, like my brother, Gerald, and my mom and Trent and my awesome husband, Keith? If this is really about thanking people, then I have to acknowledge Ross Jones, Myles McCormick, Simon Cowell, Staci Reilly, Vicki Parotino, and the countless others who helped grow a little company into something incredibly gorgeous.

Editor: Holly Dolce
Designer: Deb Wood
Production Manager: Anet Sirna-Bruder

Library of Congress Control Number: 2019939745

ISBN: 978-1-4197-4214-9
eISBN: 978-1-68335-884-8

ABRAMS The Art of Books
195 Broadway, New York, NY 10007
abramsbooks.com